MAKING ROOM FOR CHRISTMAS

TEN ORIGINAL CHRISTMAS STORIES

JOHN M. SOMMERVILLE

Making Room for Christmas: Ten Original Christmas Stories

© 2018 by John M. Sommerville

ISBN: 978-1-944298-41-8

Cover and interior design by Alan Colvin of Cue
Interior graphics by Alan Colvin of Cue
Interior production design by Niddy Griddy Design, Inc.

LCCN: 2018956776

Printed in the United States of America

1 2 3 4 5 6 7 8 9 10 Printing/Year 22 21 20 19 18

To my parents, Jim and Charlotte, who instilled in me, from a young age, a love for stories.

To my wife Kathy and daughters, Aimée and Hannah, who love all things Christmas.

And to the people of City Church who deeply love the Jesus of Christmas.

❄ ❄ ❄

CONTENTS

ACKNOWLEDGMENTS

To the people of City Church, a community of people who love God, love others and love Christmas. A special thanks to the board and staff for covering my responsibilities while I was on sabbatical the summer of 2018. Along with working on several other projects, I used the time to complete this book.

To Alan Colvin of Cue, who designed the book you hold in your hands. Alan also made a number of invaluable suggestions which have shaped the content of the book.

To Karen Pickering and the staff at Book Villages for guiding me through the process.

Finally, with deep gratitude to my wife Kathy, and daughters Aimée and Hannah, for their encouragement to see these stories in print. They have helped me each year, reading early drafts and offering suggestions including character names, a special interest of Hannah's when she was young.

INTRODUCTION

It's been many years ago now, but on a Sunday night early in December, when our daughters were young, my wife, Kathy, asked me to build a fire in the fireplace. The lights on the Christmas tree were on, and she made some hot chocolate, put a few cookies on a plate, and gathered the four of us in the living room. I read a few stories from a Christmas book, and we finished by singing a carol. It was a wonderful moment but not one we thought much about the rest of the week. Until, that is, the next Sunday night when our oldest daughter said, "Are we going to do our tradition tonight?" "What tradition?" I started to ask until I realized that she was talking about the fire in the fireplace, Christmas lights, hot chocolate, cookies, a story, and carols. I was amazed how quickly something we did just once became a "tradition." For years after, we gathered in the same way each Sunday night during the Christmas season. In the busyness of the season, it became a way for us to slow down and reflect on the message of Christmas.

A few years later we were part of starting a new church. It was, and still is, a young church, which means our Christmas Eve services are jammed with parents and their children. It didn't take more than a couple of years to realize that my carefully crafted sermons weren't connecting with the children (and probably some of their parents). So the next year I decided to try my hand at writing an original Christmas story ("A Little Christmas Miracle," the story you'll find on page 85). The response was encouraging, and so began a new tradition—this time with our church family. So, for the last decade, I've written and read a new story each Christmas Eve.

The goal each year has been to capture the spirit of Christmas in a short story accessible to everyone in the family and to engage one and all with the incarnation—God made flesh—and with Jesus's costly sacrifice, which comes to us at Christmas as a gift of hope, peace, and unquenchable joy.

For many, Christmas is the busiest time of the year. As we are swept along by the activity, it's easy to forget to pause and reflect on the meaning of the season. So consider establishing a new family tradition this Christmas. It's my prayer that these stories would help you to slow down and make room for Christmas.

THE CHRISTMAS PAGEANT
AT GATE E12

It was almost 11:00 p.m. when the show began. The waiting area outside Gate E12 had been converted into a theatre, and the young actors readied themselves for the performance. Boys and girls of all shapes and sizes were grouped in functional bundles in and around the ticket counter and the area in front of the gate. Then a confident eight-year-old girl pointed to a tall, thin man with graying hair and a clerical collar. He strode to the center of the impromptu stage, opened the book he was holding, and began to read: "In those days Caesar Augustus issued a decree that a census should be taken of the entire Roman world. (This was the first census that took place while Quirinius was governor of Syria.)"

Slowly, the eight-year-old, cloaked in a pink bathrobe with a white wool scarf wrapped around her head, made her way to the center of the stage arm in arm with a Joseph who just hours before swore he wouldn't be caught dead doing what he was about to do. Mary had a travel pillow stuffed under the robe to make it clear to all she was "great with child."

Sarah and her daughter, Olivia, had arrived at O'Hare International Airport at noon. Their flight was scheduled to leave at 3:30 p.m., but before they arrived, Sarah knew they'd be delayed. The snow had started to fall at eight in the morning, and by ten there was significant accumulation.

At three she looked out the window and saw it snowing so hard you couldn't see beyond the end of the Jetway. The weather app on her phone told her it was 10 degrees outside and dropping. She hoped they could still make it to Minneapolis yet that night.

The play's narrator continued: "And everyone went to their own town to register. So Joseph also went up from the town of Nazareth in Galilee to Judea, to Bethlehem the town of David, because he belonged to the house and line of David. He went there to register with Mary, who was pledged to be married to him and was expecting a child."

At this point, the actors came to life. Olivia, channeling her inner Mary, groaned. "Joseph," she said with great drama, "how much farther can it be? I can't take even one more step. The baby is kicking me all over."

"Just a little farther," Joseph said. Clad in an untucked blue button-down oxford shirt, he was the preppiest Joseph in dramatic history. "You can make it," he said. "I can see the star of the east just over there." He pointed to a middle school boy holding up an iPhone in flashlight mode.

The delays started the way they always do on bad-weather days at O'Hare. First, at about 3:00 p.m. the airline said the incoming flight was delayed. Then at four, air traffic control limited takeoffs and landings to one runway due to heavy snow. "Please be patient as we work to get you to your destination as quickly as possible," the harried gate agent said. In front of her a dozen angry, impatient first-class upgrade types acted as if she had ordered up the storm just to inconvenience them.

The businessman seated next to Sarah left to find something to eat at a nearby sports bar, and a minute later Sarah looked up to see an elderly black woman approaching tentatively. Her eyes asked, "Is that seat open?" Sarah smiled and invited her to sit down. "Thank you," the woman said. Just then Olivia returned from wandering the gate area. "I'm sorry," the woman said. "It looks like I took your seat, sweetheart."

"Oh no," Sarah quickly said, "she can't sit still. If she needs a seat, she can sit in my lap."

"Okay," the woman said reluctantly.

"Ma'am," Olivia said abruptly. "What's your name?"

"Eleanor," the woman said. "But you can call me Nellie."

"Are you old?" Olivia asked.

"Olivia, that's not polite," said her mother.

Nellie chuckled and said, "Yes, child, I am. Old enough to be your great-grandmother."

"You're a hundred?" Olivia asked incredulously.

Nellie laughed and said, "No, but I am eighty-seven. Born the same year as Dr. King."

Olivia was then distracted by a family with two grade school-aged boys who took seats in an adjacent section. Never one to shy away from a stranger, she went to make some new friends.

The play had reached the moment in the story when Joseph and his pregnant wife needed a hotel room. Clearly the script included some creative embellishments. Olivia had recruited some of the angry, impatient first-class upgrade types to be the innkeepers. One by one they refused the holy couple accommodations. One because a family reunion had been booked at the hotel for months. Another because Joseph didn't carry an American Express card. But finally, the manager of the cheapest hotel in Bethlehem, a Motel One, said he had a place they could use "round the back," a barn where some of the travelers had left their donkeys and horses and camels and a crocodile. The latter was the idea of a three-year-old who assumed Bethlehem was somewhere in Florida. Joseph said he thought the barn sounded quite crowded, but Mary said she thought it was just perfect as long as it had a manger.

While Olivia collected the friends who would make up the cast of the evening's play, Nellie and Sarah got to know one another.

"You traveling to see family?" Nellie asked.

"Sort of," Sarah answered. "We're spending Christmas at my ex-husband's parents' home."

"Sounds awkward," Nellie said, eyebrows raised.

"It is," Sarah answered. "But I love my in-laws. It's one of the reasons I married Jason. But since he left us, we haven't had much money and I haven't had much time. So Olivia's only seen her grandparents once in the last three years. They paid for this trip just so they could see her."

"I can see why you might be nervous, hon," Nellie said

"Who will you see?" Sarah asked, changing the subject.

"My son, James, and his family. His daughter Tonya just had a little boy, my fifth great-grandbaby."

"What did they name him?" Sarah asked.

Nellie paused. "Robert," she said. "After my late husband."

"Oh, I'm so sorry," Sarah said.

"It's okay," said Nellie. We were married for sixty-eight years. Childhood sweethearts. Met in the church choir. I miss him, but I know he'd have been proud to know there's a boy to carry on his name."

Sarah did the mental math and realized Nellie's Robert had not been gone long. Likely this was her first Christmas without him.

"Do you have other children?" Sarah asked.

"No," Nellie answered. "We just had the one boy. Strange though. Both Robert and I were from big families in Mississippi. But it took me several years to get pregnant, and then it never happened again. But he's a good boy. Worked in accounting for General Mills. Just retired last year. He's tried to get me to move up there, but I just can't leave my friends and my church."

The play's narrator continued: "While they were there, the time came for the baby to be born, and she gave birth to her firstborn, a son. She wrapped him in cloths and placed him in a manger."

The children had carefully choreographed this part of the story. Mary began to groan. Joseph called for the innkeeper and ordered him to find a doctor. They had debated the doctor part vigorously. A middle school boy who previously gave off a "too cool for Sunday School" vibe insisted it wasn't necessary. But some of the older girls thought it was essential, especially if Mary were to need a cesarean. So one of the girls went to find a real doctor in the waiting area. The young woman she found hardly looked old enough to be out of college, let alone med school. And the newly appointed on-call ob-gyn didn't have the heart to tell the cast her specialty was dermatology.

Sarah found Nellie easy to talk to. The nearly fifty-five-year gap in age seemed to help rather than hinder the conversation. A private person by nature, and particularly so since her divorce, Sarah shared with Nellie more about the past four years than she had with her own mother. She told her about Jason's infidelity. The lies. The financial deception. Then the ultimate betrayal when he announced on a Friday afternoon he was leaving her and moving to Atlanta, where he'd found a new residency.

And, he said, Anne, a woman Sarah had known well but never suspected of anything, was moving there with him. After years of working to put him through med school, she was alone. Except for four-year-old Olivia. Since then it was just the two of them.

At one point in the conversation, Sarah asked Nellie about Robert's death. "He died," she said, "back in July. We were at church. It was hot, and he was sweating. I didn't pay any attention until the pastor started to wrap up the sermon. That's when Robert slumped, his head resting on my shoulder. At first I thought he'd fallen asleep. He was eighty-eight, after all. But then I realized something was wrong. The ambulance came, but he was already gone."

"So what did you do, you know, after the funeral?" Sarah asked, stumbling over the words because she didn't know quite how to ask the question. "Oh, sometimes I feel like I'm just going through the motions. I miss him every day, and I cried for weeks. But I also have so many good memories. He was a good man, and we had many good years together. And I know I'll see him again. You see, I didn't get to say 'goodbye' to him, just 'so long.' And frankly, honey, it may not be long before I'm laid out in a pine box too. You hear me?"

Tears welled up in both their eyes. But Sarah smiled. She just loved this dear old lady. And as much as she hated the weather delay, she was glad their paths had crossed.

About this time Olivia, a bit bored and hungry, came back to her mom. The three of them agreed Sarah would go in search of food. Twenty minutes later she came back with sandwiches, chips, three bottles of water, and a few cookies.

It was then that they had a conversation which eventually led to the pageant that would cap off the evening. It started simply enough when Nellie asked Sarah and Olivia if they'd be going to church on Christmas Day. Olivia said simply, "We don't go to church."

Sarah jumped in quickly, trying to save face. "My family was never the churchgoing type," she said. "And once Jason and I got married, it just never seemed like much of a priority. Sometimes I wonder if Olivia and I should go. It certainly wouldn't hurt. But I don't know the first thing about church. I'd feel so, you know, awkward."

"You don't need to know anything, hon. Just go. Find a place that takes you as you are. Some churches are a bit stuffy. But not all of them. I think you'd love Jesus. He's all about binding up the wounds of the brokenhearted. That's you and me, honey."

Sarah smiled and cried inside a little too. Then Olivia inserted herself into the conversation. "Miss Nellie," she began, "can you explain Christmas to me? I get so confused."

Olivia insisted Nellie start from the beginning, so she told her first about Elizabeth and Zechariah and their son, John. Then she told her how the angel visited Mary. How he told her she would become pregnant with God's Son. With all the questions Olivia asked, it took a while for Nellie to get through the story. But Sarah was grateful for her daughter's inquisitiveness. She had many of the same questions but felt embarrassed to ask.

After the birth sequence, which fortunately did not require a C-section, they laid the baby in the manger, which was made up of two roller bags stacked on top of each other. At first Olivia had held out for a live baby, and there were several in the gate area. But when the mothers saw the manger, they politely declined. So they settled for a borrowed American Girl doll named Josefina. Some of the children were concerned about the gender of the baby, but they had to make do with what they had.

The idea for the pageant came about 9:00 p.m. when the Delta agent finally conceded no one would be leaving the airport that evening. Everyone had already missed their Christmas Eve plans, and now it looked like they might not be home until noon on Christmas Day. There were some unhappy travelers, but most had adjusted their expectations and resigned themselves to spending the night in the airport.

Armed with her newly acquired Bible knowledge and what looked like hours of free time, Olivia decided the children in the waiting area needed to put on a play. So she began to round up an army of actors.

Then she saw Father Pat. "Hey, mister," she said to the man with the clerical collar. "Are you God?"

"No," he laughed. "But I am a friend of His."

"Oh," she said. "Then what's your name?"

"Patrick," he said, "but most call me Father Pat."

"Father Pat," she said solemnly, "we're doing this play about Christmas. I think we'll need someone to play God. Would you do it?"

"I'd be delighted to," he said. "But I don't think you need someone to play God. Perhaps I can be your narrator."

It turned out there were lots of details to work out. The story was fuzzy in more than one of the children's minds. One of the girls wanted to know what an angel looked like. "I don't know for sure," said another. "Maybe kind of like a big white fairy."

The three boys recruited to be wise men weren't too impressed with two of the gifts. They understood gold, but frankincense and myrrh? Clearly underwhelmed, one of them said, "What about some real presents? A PlayStation or Xbox. Even some cookies or something. Don't you think Jesus would like some cookies?"

One of the shepherds said they needed names, and he had dibs on Harold. Another said he would be the German shepherd.

At one point an argument broke out about where Bethlehem was. One thought it was in Pennsylvania. Another said it was a long way away. "I think," he said, "it's in England."

"That's not right," Olivia said. "It's in the Holy Land." Although her grasp on where it was wasn't great either.

When the three of them were unable to come to an agreement, she took them to Nellie. "This lady here, she's the expert," Olivia said. "You listen to her!"

"No, children," Nellie said. "Bethlehem isn't in Pennsylvania or near London. Olivia's right. It's in the Holy Land. It's a long way off."

While Mary and Joseph gazed at the Josefina Jesus resting on top of the makeshift manger, Father Pat helped the cast transition to the next act: "There were," he read, "shepherds living out in the fields nearby, keeping watch over their flocks at night."

A single angel, dressed in a white nightgown and a white stocking cap with a red pom-pom, approached the small band of shepherds, including Harold and the German shepherd. Father Pat continued: "An angel of the Lord appeared to them, and the glory of the Lord shone around them, and they were terrified. But the angel said to them . . ." And with that, the nightgown-clad angel spoke up, assisted by a small index card in her left hand: "Do not be afraid. I bring you good news that will cause great joy for all the people. Today in the town of David a Savior has been born to you; he is the Messiah, the Lord. This will be a sign to you: You will find a baby wrapped in cloths and lying in a manger."

Then the rest of the angels, dressed in an array of bright colors and illuminated by a half a dozen smartphone flashlight apps, came from behind the ticket counter and said in unison: "Glory to God in the highest heaven, and on earth peace to those on whom his favor rests."

Then the angels returned to hide behind the ticket counter while the shepherds made the short journey to the manger and the Holy Family.

Father Pat continued his narration: "Mary treasured up all these things and pondered them in her heart."

Sarah watched her daughter gaze lovingly at the baby Jesus, and she started to tear up. The simple beauty of the story was lifting the sadness that had been her constant companion for four years. She knew then that this was a moment she, too, would treasure for the rest of her life.

The story shifted to the wise men, who brought their treasures including a half-eaten package of Oreos. "Where is the one who has been born king of the Jews?" one of them said, followed by another who said, "We saw his star when it rose and have come to worship him." The three knelt down before the child and offered their treasures to the family.

Father Pat then returned to the stage and read: "The Word became flesh and made his dwelling among us. We have seen his glory, the glory of the one and only Son, who came from the Father, full of grace and truth. To all who did receive him, to those who believed in his name, he gave the right to become children of God."

Father Pat closed his Bible and exited the stage. Uncertain if there was more, the crowd was completely quiet. Olivia, as Mary, sensed what needed to come next. She gathered the baby in her arms and, with Joseph, left the stage. The shepherds and wise men followed.

Then one, then two, then the rest of the stranded passengers began to clap. The cast returned to the stage to take their bows.

Earlier, one of the business travelers had gone down to the Cinnabon a few gates away. The employees, stuck for the night just like the rest of the travelers, agreed to make as many cinnamon rolls as they could in an hour. Another couple, aware of what he was doing, had bought as much orange juice as they could find from the various venders throughout the gate area. So when the performance ended, the Minneapolis-based flight crew sprang into action. They divided the cinnamon rolls into quarters and poured juice into small airline cups they had secured from a storage area.

By now it was nearly midnight, almost Christmas Day. Already some of the youngest among them were sleeping. The cast, heady with the success of their performance, wouldn't get tired for at least another hour. But eventually they, too, found places to sleep on benches or the floor. Space opened up so Olivia was able to sit between her mother and Nellie. She leaned against her mother's shoulder and soon fell asleep. Nellie, too, had dozed off. But Sarah sat, weary yet filled with a peace that had eluded her for years. Somehow she felt one chapter of her life had ended and another was about to begin. She felt the power of this story would do more than warm her heart; it would change her life.

LET'S TALK

1. Both Sarah and Nellie have experienced recent loss. Is there someone you know, like Sarah and Nellie, who could use some encouragement? What are one or two tangible things you might do for them this Christmas season?

2. At the end of the story, Sarah experienced a peace she'd not had in some time. She even sensed hope for the future. What is it about the Christmas story that gives you hope and peace? In what way has the Christmas story changed your life?

O LITTLE TOWN OF HOPE

It was almost midnight on December 23 when they pulled into the entrance and eased down the seventy-five yards of gravel that led to the farmhouse at the end of the drive. The anxious feeling growing in his stomach for weeks now raged out of control. With a bit of horror but little surprise, he saw the neon "vacancy" sign hanging from the side of the house. He wondered which bankrupt motel had made twenty-five dollars off his father for this treasure. He paused for a moment and glanced at the sleeping form in the passenger seat next to him. Her cashmere sweater and string of pearls revealed how out of place she was in his rusted-out 1993 brown Ford Taurus. Then again, the pearls seemed appropriate; in just moments she would find herself metaphorically "a pearl before swine."

"Lauren, we're here," he said, rousting her from a deep sleep. She smiled, unlatched the seat belt, and awkwardly began to put on her coat as she looked around at the little she could see of the house and outbuildings in the dark. Andrew was glad they'd arrived at night. He knew the morning light would erase whatever charm the homestead might have when hidden in the dark.

"Looks like someone's up," she said, noticing light streaming from the picture window at the front of the house.

"Sure does," Andrew said, hoping the number of midnight revelers was small and subdued. But almost immediately his hopes were dashed when the front door opened and Meyer family members spilled out onto the lawn wearing a collection of what normal people call ugly sweaters.

The sense of impending doom welling up in him since their 5:00 a.m. departure now occupied his full attention. Andrew had played out the probabilities in his head ever since they left Boston. There were, he figured, two possible outcomes from this visit. Either Lauren would abruptly end their relationship a day or two from now, and with Daddy's credit card, book a plane back to Philadelphia as quickly as possible. Or, in the absolute best scenario he could let himself imagine, she would grin and bear it, only to demand five minutes into their drive back to Boston that as long as they were together, she would never again travel east of the Allegheny Mountains. He couldn't imagine she'd find anything remotely charming about his family.

Andrew's mom arrived first and opened the passenger door. Lauren stepped out and extended her hand, but to Andrew's dismay his mom gave her a bear hug that lifted her off her feet. "Sweetheart, you're just as pretty as I imagined you'd be," she said. "Boomer," she snapped, "don't just stand there; get the kids' bags. Let's get them out of the cold."

The whole army of Meyers grabbed what they could find in the car and headed into the house. Mugs of hot chocolate magically appeared, and the inquisition began. Soon Lauren poured out her life story. She had been raised in the Philadelphia suburb of Bryn Mawr along the Main Line, a series of wealthy suburbs extending out from the center of the historic city. She had attended The Baldwin School, a private academy for girls. It was the sort of place with an application process that mimics what it takes to get into an Ivy League school. Andrew was certain she had had to ace the preschool version of the SAT just to get in. Lauren's father, a Yale Law School grad, worked for a firm in the city, and the family lived in a three-story Georgian mansion of the sort that could well have served as the summer home of Benjamin Franklin. As she told her story, Andrew wondered if his family had any comprehension of how different their world was from Lauren's.

Andrew had gone home with her for Thanksgiving, and the visit had gone fairly well. He'd been able to hide his rural Illinois roots enough to survive, but he had the clear sense he lacked the pedigree Mr. and Mrs. Brooks had hoped for. They were cordial enough but probably assumed the relationship wouldn't last. Now, as Lauren got full-on exposure to the Meyer family, he was convinced they were probably right.

After the Thanksgiving visit to Philadelphia, Lauren had invited herself home with him for Christmas. When she first suggested the idea, he told her no, it was out of the question. When she asked again, he offered a couple of lame excuses, which she quickly rebutted. When she didn't drop the subject, he wondered if this was a plot her mother had hatched to help her daughter see his unsuitability. When he suggested as much, she promptly and indignantly denied it. Because Lauren was essentially guileless, he believed her and consented to the plan, immediately regretting this moment of weakness.

Ever since, he'd tried to prepare her for what lay ahead. However, it was impossible to come up with adjectives clever enough to put a positive spin on a family most would simply describe as weird. He tried anyway and told her the Meyers were enthusiastic, but eccentric; creative, if slightly unconventional; and sensitive, bordering on sentimental. He didn't want to scare her away entirely, but she needed to be prepared for what he believed was the oddest family subculture in Western civilization.

When the group ran out of questions, Andrew's dad brought an end to the festivities. "All right, everyone, it's time to get a little power nap. We've got a lot to do in the morning." When his mom began assigning bedrooms, Andrew realized his dad had carried through on a plan he'd hatched several years ago. In past years, when Uncle Jake and Aunt Nancy came for the holidays, they had stayed in a Super 8 fifteen miles away in Decatur. But apparently, while Andrew had been away at school, his dad had converted the loft in the garage into what he now called "the bunkhouse." The guys would sleep there, and the women would double up in the house. To his shock, his mom had paired Lauren with Granny Gert on the hide-a-bed in the den. "Mom," Andrew whispered to her. "She snores!"

"Oh, I almost forgot," she said, grabbing Lauren by the arm and digging for something in her sweater pocket. "You'll need these." Then she pressed a small packet of reusable earplugs into Lauren's palm. Andrew looked away, afraid to see the reaction on Lauren's face. Swept along by the moving tide of bodies, he found himself in the bunkhouse, watching cousins fight over who got to sleep on the top bunks. He chose a bottom bunk in the corner and crawled in while a series of farts and corresponding guffaws bounced around the room. His older brother and uncle began to give him grief over Lauren. "Scoot," Uncle Jake said, "you better lock that down soon before she has second thoughts."

"Yeah, Scooter," his brother said, "you mess this up, and you'll regret it for the rest of your life."

That's right, Andrew thought. *And if I can minimize the damage all of you can do, maybe I'll have a shot.*

It was about 2:00 a.m. when everything settled down and everyone in the bunkhouse was asleep—except Andrew. He lay looking up at the slats of the bed above him and wondered how it would go in the morning. He resolved to wake early so he could protect Lauren from the frenetic activity that generally consumed a day at the Meyer homestead.

When he awoke, the sun was higher in the sky than he would have liked. He looked at his watch; it was already 8:30 a.m. He quickly brushed his teeth in the communal bathroom his dad had built just below the loft. He put on a baseball cap to hide his bedhead and made his way to the house. It was empty. A note on the counter said the ladies had gone to Decatur to make a Walmart run. Andrew doubted Lauren had ever been to a Walmart. Years before, he recalled how the entire family could hardly contain their excitement when the store first opened. But he doubted Lauren's first visit to Walmart held any of the allure his did.

Just then his dad stepped into the room. He slipped off his coat and boots and joined Andrew at the counter. "How about a sticky bun, Scoot?" he said. Andrew took a knife and cut one of the gooey caramel rolls out of the pan on the counter and put it on a plate. He cut another for himself, and they both dug in.

Andrew's dad had lived in Hope, Illinois, population 1,200, nearly his whole life. Only the four years he spent in Champaign-Urbana to get his degree from the U of I in Mechanical Engineering had taken him away. Upon graduation he'd found a job in nearby Decatur with a food processing company. A few months later he'd fallen in love with Andrew's mom, Julie, who had moved to Hope the year before to teach math at Hope High. The two married the next year, and the first of their four children arrived almost a year to the day after their first anniversary. In the next five years two more children arrived, followed by a six-year gap when the baby of the family, a little girl, arrived.

"How's school?" his dad asked.

"Great. It's hard, but I love it." Andrew and his dad had different temperaments but shared a love for all things mechanical. His dad was a mechanical whiz. In Decatur, he quickly rose up the ranks until he was the lead engineer at the plant. He'd been offered numerous promotions, but each time he refused. He had no interest in moving and liked the rhythm of his life. He left the house each day at 6:00 a.m. and made the fifteen-mile drive to Decatur. Once there, he worked hard all day, but at 3:30 p.m. he was out the door. Once home he napped an hour, got up in time for the evening meal, and then went to the garage, a kid or two in tow, to work on whatever project caught his fancy.

The family lived on a small hobby farm a mile outside of Hope. His dad bought the place—a house, barn, and forty acres—when Andrew was eight. The next year he built a large addition off the back, doubling the size of the farmhouse. Then he added a large outbuilding, which served as both a garage and a shop for his many mechanical projects.

Over the years he had built an ultralight aircraft of his own design and a series of go-carts Smoke raced at area tracks, and he restored an Oscar Mayer Wienermobile he found for sale in the classifieds in a Kentucky newspaper. The connection to the family surname, despite the different spelling, made the deal too tempting. When the vehicle was operational, Andrew's older brother Smoke used it regularly on dates, but when Andrew turned sixteen, he chose to postpone dating rather than show up at his date's door in such a memorable mode of transportation.

A serial inventor, Andrew's dad held nearly a hundred patents, most from work projects, but an additional dozen came from projects conceived and developed in the garage. Only two had proved commercially viable. One, a custom garage door system that made the door look like the rest of the house, never quite caught on, perhaps because it still seemed odd to have a driveway that ran up to the side of the house. The second idea was more profitable. It consisted of a platform a homeowner could lower to the floor, drive on a lawn tractor or motorcycle, and then press a button, and a lift mechanism would take the item up for storage as high as ten feet off the floor. The system was sturdy, reliable, and cost-effective, and during the last five years it had generated enough cash flow to keep the kids in college.

"Well, Scooter," his dad said, washing down the caramel stuck to his teeth with some lukewarm black coffee. "We've got some work to do. How about you and Smoke get some hay bales and make some benches in the back of the wagon? Banana's having some friends over tonight for a hayride."

While Andrew and Lauren made the drive the day before from Boston, he had explained to her the family's fondness for nicknames. It all started with his dad. He might be Bob at work in Decatur, but in Hope everyone simply called him Boomer. The name came from the time in high school when he had buried a weather balloon at the center of a rival school's football field. Then, with a radio-controlled remote, he had detonated several small charges to allow the balloon to inflate with the words *Lions Rule* painted on the side. Because the device had been buried so deeply, the referees ruled the field unplayable and suspended the game until the next afternoon to make the necessary repairs. Mr. Manning, the school's principal, thought the stunt was clever and decided to leave well enough alone. But everyone knew who was responsible, so it wasn't long before even Mr. Manning was calling Andrew's dad Boomer.

His dad loved nicknames and scattered them liberally on all his friends and acquaintances. A high school friend was Rip, from the time his jeans split down the middle when he bent over to pick up a dropped biology textbook. Andrew's mom, Julie, became Jewels; his older brother, Robert, was Smoke, after he set part of a neighbor's cornfield on fire. His older sister, Sarah, they called Bunny, after a stuffed rabbit she carried with her everywhere until she was six; and his youngest sister, Hannah, became, well, Banana.

His siblings seemed okay with the nickname deal, but in high school Andrew decided it was undignified and began to call his siblings by their proper names. The rest of the family humored him but also accused him of putting on airs. What he hated most was his own nickname. Drew or even Andy would have been fine, but at home everyone called him Scooter. He hadn't walked until he was sixteen months old because he had figured out how to efficiently scoot around on his bottom wherever he wanted to go. It wasn't until the family installed wall-to-wall carpet that walking even made sense. Now, almost twenty years later, he couldn't shake the name.

The rest of the morning they prepared for the Christmas Eve and Christmas Day festivities. The hayride, turkey bowling, and a fireworks show all had to be arranged. The fireworks had always seemed to Andrew like a bridge too far, but several years before, his dad had persuaded the pastor of their church that if fireworks were suitable for the Fourth of July, then a short show after the Christmas Eve service was a fitting way to send folks home. The pastor always made what seemed to Andrew a tenuous connection between Roman candles and the angels who appeared to the shepherds.

29

By lunchtime all was under control. The women arrived back from their trip to Decatur with bags of goodies from Walmart and the Dollar Tree. Andrew expected Lauren to have a pained look on her face, but she seemed cheerful enough. Without hesitation she jumped in and helped the rest of the women get a lunch of sandwiches, chips, and cookies on the table. In a matter of minutes the table was awash in conversation. With shock he realized Lauren now had a nickname of her own—Ralph, as in, you guessed it, Ralph Lauren.

An hour later, lunch finished and the dishes put away, Lauren asked if there was anything else she could do. "No, sweetheart. Why don't you kids go for a drive? I'm sure Scooter would love to show you the town."

"No, Mom," Andrew answered. "There's nothing to see."

"But I want to see the town," Lauren said. "I need to see all these places everyone's been talking about."

Andrew thought about asking what she'd been told but decided to leave well enough alone. He helped her with her coat and then grabbed his, and they made their way to the Taurus and took the mile journey into town. Along the way she made him point out the field where his dad had mowed the letters M.I.T. into a hayfield the day Andrew had been accepted. The women even told her that his dad had then gone up in the ultralight to take a picture of the field and sent it in to the local weekly paper. At the time Andrew wished he had chosen Rensselaer Polytechnic Institute to make his dad work a little harder to get all the letters in.

He showed her the school he'd gone to from kindergarten all the way through high school. Then they drove by the hardware store where he'd worked on Saturdays during high school. They walked both sides of the one-block downtown and peeked in the little town library he'd spent so many hours in as a child. Then he took her to see the small city park he had so loved as a child, the old locomotive at one end and the band shell where he'd played his trumpet with the band at the other.

They drove back to the house in time to change clothes and caravan to the church for the 4:00 p.m. Christmas Eve service. Andrew thought the pastor gave one of his better Christmas Eve sermons. "The first Christmas," he said, "wasn't much like the fairy tale we often make it out to be. But the message is one of good news for all people—rich and poor, young and old, skeptic and seeker alike. It was fitting, then, that Jesus was placed in a manger, a feed trough, where the animals ate." Later, he told them, Jesus described Himself as the bread of life, promising to satisfy the deepest hunger and longings of our souls. "What we hunger for," he said, "can't be found under a Christmas tree. Forgiveness, meaning, life purpose, and a love that won't let us go—these can only be found in Jesus." Then he closed with an invitation to everyone to come to the stable and satisfy the deepest desires of their hearts.

After a rousing rendition of "Joy to the World," the entire congregation went out into the parking lot while Boomer lived up to his nickname and set off a seven-minute display of fireworks several said was the best yet. Then it was back to the house for Christmas Eve dinner, followed by the final night of yet one more family tradition—the Meyer Family Christmas Film Festival. This retrospective look at holiday films began on Thanksgiving Day with *Planes, Trains and Automobiles* and progressed through classics such as *Miracle on 34th Street*, *Elf*, *Home Alone* and *Home Alone 2*, and finally concluded on Christmas Eve with *It's a Wonderful Life*.

Halfway through the movie, Andrew left Lauren with his youngest sister and made his way into the empty living room. A few minutes later Aunt Nancy came in. "Mind if I join you?" she asked.

"Not at all," he said.

"I can tell you're a bit nervous. Worried whether she'll turn and run after a week with the Meyers, aren't you?"

Aunt Nancy was the person in the family he related to best. She'd grown up in suburban Chicago and had always lived in or near a city until she met Andrew's uncle in college. "I think I know a bit of what you're feeling," she said. "This family's an acquired taste. I remember the first time I came here. I was two hundred miles from Chicago, but it might as well have been two thousand. The world around us is changing, but this place seems to stay pretty much the same."

She paused for few moments, then continued. "I know what you're thinking. She's faking it; that the moment you get back in the car to Boston, she'll tell you she's never coming back to Hope. But you're wrong. Andrew, you'll never live here again. You're not wired for small-town life. Your mom and dad know that, and they're okay with it. But you need to remember the good that comes with this place.

"I think you'll be surprised by Lauren's reaction to Hope. I've only had a few hours with her, but I think she appreciates the values this family represents. If she's anything like I was, I imagine her family is a bit stuffy, even pretentious. There's none of that here. In a funny way, coming here is like visiting a foreign country. It's exotic, even charming. And in small doses, it can be a lot of fun. And there's no one quite like your dad. Who else constructs a real medieval fort for his kids, complete with a catapult? Or builds an ultralight aircraft so you boys can drop bowling balls on junked cars from five hundred feet? Or makes spud guns out of PVC pipe and borrows his wife's hairspray to shoot potatoes at the mailbox at the end of the driveway?

"You've always been such an earnest kid. For the most part it's served you well. And I'm glad you're anxious, because it shows you care about her. I think she senses it and finds it reassuring. I can tell she likes you, and if you get that far, you'll be good for each other—the Harvard English major and the M.I.T. mechanical engineer. Just don't ever get so stuffy you forget where you're from. Okay, Scooter?"

"Okay," Andrew answered.

"Now get back in there. I think Clarence is about to get his wings."

Andrew made his way back into the family room. Lauren and twelve-year-old Hannah made room for him. With Lauren on one side and Hannah on the other, they nestled in and watched as George Bailey came to understand how good he had it in Bedford Falls.

As the movie credits rolled, Andrew's mind wandered back to the pastor's sermon. He thought again about the Holy Family in the stable on the first Christmas. The pastor was right. Life is seldom like a fairy tale. But if life turns out anything like what happened in the little town of Bethlehem, everything else will fall into place. Andrew trusted it would and felt at peace.

LET'S TALK

1. Andrew felt uncomfortable bringing Lauren to meet his eccentric family. Have you ever felt awkward around someone? What did they do, or what do you wish they would have done, to help you feel comfortable? What can you do to help others feel more comfortable in situations where they may feel awkward?

2. The pastor at Andrew's church said the Christmas story was no fairy tale—that Jesus was born in humble circumstances. How does Jesus's humble background help you relate to Him? What does this tell you about His character? How does knowing He experienced what we have help you understand how He can help you with whatever you face?

PRINCESS OF PEACE

Scott rolled to a stop in front of the tidy two-story white house. He grabbed the duffel bag out of the trunk and walked up the steps to the wraparound porch dominating the front of the house. Gently he knocked on the door.

He was greeted not by his mother, as he had expected, but by a barefoot four-foot-tall princess complete with a faux silver and rhinestone tiara. "Uncle Scott!" little Maggie screamed and ran toward the kitchen to get her grandmother, leaving Scott standing on the front porch. Drying her hands on a towel, his mother made her way to the door. Smiling the best he could, he stepped in, hugged her, and then squatted down to greet little Maggie, who threw her arms around his neck with characteristic six-year-old enthusiasm. Looking around, he saw things were much as they had been every Christmas since he could remember. His mother had a deft touch; everything looked so festive and warm that it was hard not to be drawn in and comforted.

"How was your drive?" his sister, Katy, asked, coming in from the kitchen.

"Fine," said Scott. "Glad I left a day early. I hear snow is on the way."

The day before, Scott had left New York City during the morning rush hour, guiding his red BMW Z4 through the Holland Tunnel and northwest across New Jersey toward Pennsylvania, through Ohio, and on to Indiana. He'd visualized the drive before but never under these circumstances; the sun wasn't shinning, the top wasn't down, and the passenger seat was empty.

One week ago, the plan had been to take a two-hour flight from LaGuardia, rent a car, and arrive in time to meet everyone for the Christmas Eve service at Christ Church. But that was before he was unexpectedly unemployed and emotionally adrift. In past years he'd arrive at the last minute as the conquering hero, only to rush out a couple of days later to ski in Switzerland or surf on Saint Barts. Humbled, he thought about staying in New York, but he knew he needed to make an appearance at home.

On December 15, Scott had been part of an RIF, a reduction in force, he never saw coming. For eleven years, he'd scratched and clawed his way up to partner at a Wall Street bank. Leveraging an exceptional capacity with numbers, he'd transformed his slightly geeky high school persona into a clever, confident financial whiz, with an almost unbroken string of success. But that was last week.

"Uncle Scott," Maggie blurted, standing in front of the living room picture window. "Is that your toy car?"

"Maggie," his sister corrected, "it's not a toy; it's a sports car."

"Uncle Scott, can I have a ride?"

"Sweetheart, let your uncle settle in first," Katy said as Scott picked up his duffel bag and started up the stairs to his old room on the second floor. Maggie followed, pink Cinderella dress swishing with each step they took up the L-shaped staircase. Talking a mile a minute, she touched on topic after topic, ending with what she wanted for Christmas.

Thirteen hours in the car had been good for Scott. Alone with his thoughts, he had driven the route his family had traveled when he headed east for his freshman year of college. At the time, they didn't know it would be their last family trip. Later in the fall, Scott's father collapsed just outside his office at the small Presbyterian college he'd taught at for thirty-five years. Scott had rushed home, numb to the reality that at eighteen he'd never see his father again. Katy cried so much that friends and family worried about her, but it was Scott they should have paid attention to.

Katy felt things deeply, but it didn't deter her from loving again, hoping always for the best despite the circumstances. Scott's stoicism masked a deep pain that made him reluctant to give himself so fully to anyone again. The more you love, the more vulnerable you become. The more you hope, the more open to disappointment you are. Without him realizing it, his heart began to shrivel behind a protective wall quickly erected to insulate him from pain. He was under no illusions his work was fulfilling or even meaningful. But it filled a void and gave an outward veneer of respectability that kept people from asking what was going on inside.

As he drove, the empty passenger seat reminded him of how alone he felt. The sting of a recently failed relationship was only part of it. They were two self-absorbed people looking more for what they could get than what they could give, so it was inevitable the arrangement would be abandoned when the novelty wore off and other priorities intervened. Scott was less disappointed it ended than by his own failure to feel.

What he missed most was his father, the gentle philosopher who, while different from his son in temperament, understood Scott and made him feel safe in a world where even the outward trappings of success had failed to rid him of fear. Professor Campbell was strong but vulnerable, a man who had held on to hope in spite of his own disappointments. He was unjaded and retained an implicit trust in humanity. Most significant to Scott, his father had committed his faith, hope, and love to his son, whose joy he coveted most. The irony, Scott recognized, was that in an effort to protect himself from pain, he'd built a respectable but joyless life that would have grieved his father.

After he was back downstairs, little Maggie disappeared only to emerge from the kitchen carrying her boots and coat. "Let's go for a ride," she announced. The smiling royalty quickly pushed her bare feet into the fur-lined boots and her arms into an orange and blue hand-me-down ski jacket that clashed with her pink dress. Scott grabbed his coat and keys, and they headed out the front door. Maggie bounded down the steps, running awkwardly in her boots to the car as fast as she could.

Now that he was at home, the car embarrassed him. It was an impulse purchase two years earlier, an obvious symbol of conspicuous consumption sure to be understood by everyone in this town as an immature attempt to buy an identity. He could just hear a neighbor or two saying, "Who does he think he is anyway?" And they'd be right. He had thought about stopping along the way to rent one of those generic American sedans so common in midwestern small towns. But he knew it would only be a smoke screen for the fact that, BMW or not, something was amiss. He might as well own up to it and not try to bluff his way through this uncomfortable reality.

As Scott started the engine, Maggie asked if they could put the top down. "But it's freezing outside," he protested.

"Just turn the heat up," Maggie countered. Scott couldn't argue with such impeccable logic, so he flipped the switch and waited as the motor lifted the top up and folded it back into the compartment behind the seats. "Let's go!" Maggie shouted, and off they went, a stream-of-consciousness commentary coming from the passenger seat as she looked around the cockpit of the car, asking what every knob and button did.

They drove past the familiar landmarks that dotted the way to the town center. The blanket of snow made everything look like a postcard. They turned left and made their way past the park with a gazebo where he'd played his saxophone with the high school band at Fourth of July celebrations. Two blocks south they came to the edge of the twenty-acre MacPherson College campus founded in the late nineteenth century by the Scottish Presbyterians who settled in this small Indiana town. They passed the familiar brick buildings of the college, then the football stadium with "Terriers" emblazoned over a background of black watch plaid.

Predictably, both Scott and Maggie were thoroughly frozen from the waist up while their feet were practically on fire. Maggie went on telling him about her school friends, even the boys, though she thought they were mostly dumb and gross, something Scott knew was probably true.

"Hey, Uncle Scott," Maggie said, her face lighting up like she'd just thought up the vision for Disneyland, "can we show your car to my friends?"

"Sure," Scott said, unsure whether or not this was wise. The problem, he soon discovered, was Maggie knew what her friends' houses looked like; she just couldn't tell him where they were. Fast thinking on Maggie's part saved the day. She grabbed his iPhone, called her mother, and soon had directions, first to Lindsey's, then Betsy's, then Lucy's, and finally to Jack's. At each house, Maggie showed off his car, and the two kids would scrunch close together in the passenger seat for a ride around the block. Jack was the only one to ask him to peel out, something Scott declined. An hour and a half later, just as the promised snow began to fall, the two of them arrived back home with cheeks pink enough to suggest they'd spent the time skating in the park.

Scott and Katy shared hot chocolate and cookies in the living room while their mom bustled about in the kitchen getting dinner ready so it'd be on the table when Katy's husband, Rob, arrived after basketball practice. "How are you doing?" she asked.

"Fine," he answered. "It was a little unexpected, but things are tough everywhere. How are you?" In the back-and-forth Scott asked most of the questions so he wouldn't have to answer any. It was a bit jarring for his sister, who was used to a brother who normally had a hard time talking about anything but himself. Katy gave him an update on her job at the college and Rob's at the high school. Rob taught history and coached the boys' basketball team. She told Scott it looked like they had a good team this year. His best player was getting the attention of a few colleges in the area.

When Rob walked in the back door, they made their way to the dining room table for dinner. Maggie insisted on sitting next to Uncle Scott and offered a prayer that included a petition for a white-bearded, portly gentleman she knew would leave the next day on a long journey toward her midwestern town.

After dessert, Katy and Rob started to pack up when Maggie had yet another brilliant idea. "Mom, can I have a sleepover with Uncle Scott?" What ensued next, which anyone with a six-year-old can vividly imagine, was a verbal negotiation with dubious logic. Finally, realizing she had lost the battle, she switched strategies and asked if she could spend the next night, Christmas Eve, at Grandma's with Uncle Scott. Softened by the previous request, mother and grandmother looked at each other and gave in—to shrieks of delight. After they'd said their goodbyes, the house grew quiet for the first time since Scott had arrived six hours earlier. He helped his mother with the dishes. Then she warmed some cider, and they sat in the living room and watched the snow fall outside through the window. His mother offered updates on family friends Scott vaguely remembered, but they were both tired from the day's activities and turned in early.

Scott awoke early the next morning to a clear blue sky; the sun shone unimpeded on a diamond-encrusted surface of pure white. He pulled on a down jacket hanging in the closet and went downstairs. Slipping into an old pair of his father's SORELs, he went out the back door to retrieve a snow shovel from the garage. As a child, he'd cursed the long driveway that stretched from the front to nearly the back of the lot, but today he enjoyed clearing the snow from the drive and the sidewalk out front.

More than an hour later, snow still clinging to his extremities, he sat down with his mother at the kitchen table to a breakfast of scrambled eggs, bacon, and freshly baked coffeecake. She thanked him for shoveling, and he quizzed her on gift ideas for Katy, Rob, and Maggie, surprised by the simple, inexpensive ideas his mother suggested. In the past, he'd brought lavish gifts his assistant had purchased for him at exclusive Fifth Avenue shops. It slowly dawned on him he'd been burdening his family with a puzzling array of expensive white elephants, leaving them with the moral dilemma of wondering if they could return the items for cash and buy something more useful without him noticing. They might as well, he thought; his old assistant might remember what she purchased, but he couldn't.

After breakfast, he borrowed his mother's Impala—in the snow the Z4 wouldn't have made it to the stop sign at the corner—and drove to Walmart, the one new development in town since he'd left nineteen years earlier. Just a week before, Scott wouldn't have been caught dead in a Walmart, even though he had a thousand shares of its stock in his portfolio. Arbitrarily, he set a spending limit: $75 per person. It wasn't for frugality's sake, although he knew he'd need to start watching his pennies; it was principle. Anything more seemed inappropriate. Forty-five minutes later he walked out with a sixteen-piece white ceramic dinnerware set for Katy, a Black and Decker rechargeable drill with accessories for Rob, a West Bend bread maker for his mother, and a long royal blue church coat with black buttons and a sash for Maggie. Once he was back home, his mother helped him wrap the gifts and place them under the tree.

At three thirty, they quickly changed into church clothes and made the five-minute drive to Christ Church. As they entered the sanctuary, Maggie spotted her uncle and rushed down the aisle, took his hand, and guided him to the seat she'd saved for him on the fourth row. She had traded in the pink princess dress for a black velvet long-sleeved dress layered with a ballerina-like mesh overskirt, black tights, and patent-leather dress shoes. Her hair was neatly tied up with a red ribbon.

The front of the church was dominated by the half-life-sized crèche with carved and painted figures of the entire cast from the Christmas story. They were early enough that Maggie was able to lead Uncle Scott to see the scene up close. Excitedly she pointed out each character by name, as though it were the first time he'd ever been to church. At least recently, Scott thought, her intuition was correct.

The service began with the choir proceeding from the back, candles in hand, singing "O Come, All Ye Faithful." Readings and more carols followed, leaving Scott with a simultaneous mixture of longing and regret. When the minister made his way to the lectern, Maggie nestled in next to him, her feet dangling and moving back and forth, the sheen of the patent leather bouncing up on the pew in front of them.

The minister began with the words of Isaiah 9: "For to us a child is born, to us a son is given, and the government will be on his shoulders. And he will be called Wonderful Counselor, Mighty God, Everlasting Father, Prince of Peace." Scott listened as the minister turned to Luke 2 and concluded with the words the angel spoke to the shepherds: "'Do not be afraid. I bring you good news that will cause great joy for all the people. Today in the town of David a Savior has been born to you; he is the Messiah, the Lord. This will be a sign to you: You will find a baby wrapped in cloths and lying in a manger.' Suddenly a great company of the heavenly host appeared with the angel, praising God and saying, 'Glory to God in the highest heaven, and on earth peace to those on whom his favor rests.'"

Scott's attention drifted in and out as the minister talked about the Prince of Peace, the Savior who arrived as a baby the first Christmas Day. He told them peace was not just the absence of conflict, but something much greater. It was order, well-being, safety, harmony, and happiness—the longing we all have for a world that works the way we know it should. Jesus came, he said, to make things right in our lives and in the world. "Most of you," he said, "have probably never said no to Jesus, but you haven't exactly said yes either. This Christmas, make room in your hearts for Him."

As the minister returned to his seat, the choir stood, organ music filled the room, and together everyone sang, "Joy to the world, the Lord is come; let earth receive her King; let every heart prepare him room, and heaven and nature sing." Maggie stood proudly by her uncle, singing at the top of her voice. She only knew the first verse, so she sang the same words through for all four verses, eliciting a few chuckles from the family seated in the third row.

Back home after the service, the smell of ham and scalloped potatoes and green bean casserole filled the room. The Christmas dishes shone on a red tablecloth accented by the white tapered candles burning brightly from the center. As they began to eat, Scott felt the melancholy lifting. He watched his sister with admiration. Her joy and contentment with life made him jealous. Maggie kept things lively, objecting only when her mother insisted she eat at least three green beans. Then came the pumpkin pie with a dollop of Cool Whip on top.

Finally it was Maggie's bedtime. Scott's mom got out a small plate and a glass they'd used since he was Maggie's age and told her to choose a few cookies for Santa. Then they filled the glass with milk and placed the milk and cookies on the mantle over the fireplace. Katy took Maggie upstairs to get her into her pink princess pajamas. Maggie insisted Uncle Scott join her for prayers in her mother's old bedroom. Then they shut the door and left her tossing and turning with clear instructions not to wake anyone before seven in the morning—difficult words for an overly excited child who had just learned to tell time.

Not too much later, Scott made his way to bed. Alone with his thoughts, it felt like the sense of hopelessness he'd had when he left New York was beginning to lift. However, he, too, tossed and turned, uncertain what would follow once the peaceful bubble of this holiday had ended. He'd been in bed for about two hours when he got up and went back downstairs. As long as he could remember, his mother had left the tree lit all night on Christmas Eve. He made his way into the living room and noticed she'd taken the obligatory bites out of the cookies and a sip from the glass of milk Maggie had left for Santa. Then he headed to the kitchen, poured a small glass of eggnog, returned to the living room, added a log to the fire, and sat down.

Staring at the tree, he was alone with his thoughts when he heard a creak on the stairs. Looking up he saw the outline of a small princess making her way down the stairs, a white threadbare blanket in hand. Maggie made her way into the room and sat down on the couch beside her uncle. "What are you doing up?" Scott asked.

"I was worried Santa wouldn't come." The bites in the cookies and the extra presents his mother had left under the tree proved her fears were groundless. "Are you having a hard time waiting for morning too?" Maggie asked.

"I guess so," said Scott with a smile.

The two of them sat there for a few more minutes before Maggie broke the silence. "Uncle Scott," she said, "are you sad?"

"Why do you ask?" he replied.

"Well, Mom said you can't work and don't have a family."

Scott paused, chuckling at her directness but also amazed at the sensitivity of this six-year-old. "I'm a little sad," he said. "But being with you has cheered me up."

"Good," she said. "Mom told me I wasn't supposed to bring up the sad stuff, but I just don't want you to be sad anymore."

"Thanks, Maggie" was all Scott could think of to say. Maggie pulled his arm around her shoulder and pressed a cheek against his chest. Scott sipped the eggnog until it was gone. It wasn't long before he realized Maggie had fallen asleep. He waited a bit longer, then gathered her in his arms, carried her to her bed, tucked her in, and closed the door.

He returned to his room, climbed into bed, and pulled the covers up just under his chin. Soon he, too, began to doze off as the sights, sounds, smells, and words of the day echoed in his head: "Wonderful Counselor, Mighty God, Everlasting Father, Prince of Peace."

LET'S TALK

1. Scott arrives home feeling sad. He's just lost his job and isn't sure what to do next. How does his niece, Maggie, cheer him up? How can you cheer someone up like Maggie did?

2. The pastor called Jesus "the Prince of Peace." What is it is about being home again that brings Scott peace? The pastor ended his sermon by inviting those who lack peace in their lives to make room in their hearts for Jesus. In what area of life are you lacking peace? How can you make room in your heart for Jesus?

IVY'S CHRISTMAS VISITORS

Once upon a time in a faraway land there lived a poor woodcutter and his only daughter. They lived in a small cottage on the edge of a large forest in the north of the country. The girl's mother died shortly after giving birth to her daughter. For six years, Thomas had raised this beloved girl whom his wife had named Ivy just moments before she took her last breath.

Times were hard, but Ivy had a knack for making the most of whatever came their way. Each evening she prepared their meager meal, and before they ate, they thanked God for providing what they needed for the day.

Thomas loved his daughter dearly. She had her mother's kind and sensitive heart, and as she grew, he marveled at her beauty and grace. He prayed that in time she would find a loving husband with whom she might have a family. But for now he contented himself with their simple life together.

As Christmas approached, life in the cottage grew grim. After an unusually hot and dry summer, what they had stored in the rafters of the cottage was less than they usually had at this time of the year. And to make matters worse, the heat of summer had given way to an unusually cold and snowy winter. Thomas found it increasingly difficult to cut, gather, and deliver all the firewood required to keep the homes in the area warm against the cold north wind.

On Christmas Eve, while Thomas was delivering wood, Ivy prepared the evening meal. A clever girl, she had saved a few treats for their Christmas Day dinner, so the evening meal was a simple affair: a small loaf of bread, some cheese, and two small bowls of potato soup.

The two sat down to eat their dinner, aware that soon even the small amount they had would be gone. But they pushed the thought from their minds and ate what they had before them.

When they had finished and the dishes has been cleaned and put away, Thomas went to a shelf on the wall and pulled down the family Bible. Opening the well-worn book, he read aloud the story of the birth of Jesus. Ivy listened as her father read the words of the familiar story: "And it came to pass in those days, that there went out a decree from Caesar Augustus that all the world should be taxed. . . And all went to be taxed, every one into his own city. And Joseph also went up from Galilee, out of the city of Nazareth, into Judaea, unto the city of David, which is called Bethlehem; (because he was of the house and lineage of David) to be taxed with Mary his espoused wife, being great with child."

"Father," Ivy interrupted, as she often did when he read to her, "do you think they were cold?" Her eyes wandered to the window and the wind-whipped white landscape just outside their door.

"Perhaps," he answered, turning back to the words on the page.

"And," said Ivy, interrupting again, "do you think they had enough to eat?"

"I hope so," he answered.

"Oh, Father," Ivy said, "if only they had come here; we would have given them something to eat. And they could have warmed at our fire."

"Yes," her father replied, smiling at his kind-hearted daughter.

Turning back to the story, he read on. "And so it was, that, while they were there, the days were accomplished that she should be delivered. And she brought forth her firstborn son, and wrapped him in swaddling clothes, and laid him in a manger; because there was no room for them in the inn."

"Father," Ivy again interrupted, "if only they had come here, we would have given them a place to stay."

"Yes, I suppose we would have," Thomas said as he looked around and wondered where they would find room for three more to sleep in the small one-room cottage.

She must have read his mind and quickly added, "Jesus could have my bed, and Mary and Joseph yours."

"And where would we sleep?" he asked.

"In the stable," she answered. Thomas smiled, wondering how cold it was in the simple lean-to attached to the back of the cottage where their two goats huddled near the dwindling stack of hay he had cut last summer.

Thomas continued to read: "And there were in the same country shepherds abiding in the field, keeping watch over their flock by night." Ivy's eyes widened as he read, "And, lo, the angel of the Lord came upon them, and the glory of the Lord shone round about them: and they were sore afraid. And the angel said unto them, Fear not: for, behold, I bring you good tidings of great joy, which shall be to all people. For unto you is born this day in the city of David a Saviour, which is Christ the Lord. And this shall be a sign unto you; ye shall find the babe wrapped in swaddling clothes, lying in a manger. And suddenly there was with the angel a multitude of the heavenly host praising God, and saying, Glory to God in the highest, and on earth peace, good will toward men. And it came to pass, as the angels were gone away from them into heaven, the shepherds said one to another, Let us now go even unto Bethlehem, and see this thing which is come to pass, which the Lord hath made known unto us. And they came with haste, and found Mary, and Joseph, and the babe lying in a manger."

"Father," Ivy burst in, "would we have gone to see the baby?"

"Yes," he answered. "I suppose we would have."

"Oh," she said, "I wish I could have heard the angels sing and seen the baby Jesus." Thomas watched as Ivy, eyes wide open, imagined her way into Luke's story. But soon her attention returned.

"Father," she said, "read to me about the wise men." So Thomas turned back in his Bible to Matthew and read the story of the kings who came to Herod and asked, "Where is he that is born King of the Jews? for we have seen his star in the east, and are come to worship him."

Ivy listened as the wise men traveled to Bethlehem, where the star stopped at the house where Joseph and Mary were staying with the baby. She listened to how, "when they saw the star, they rejoiced with exceeding great joy. And when they were come into the house, they saw the young child with Mary his mother, and fell down, and worshipped him: and when they had opened their treasures, they presented unto him gifts; gold, and frankincense and myrrh."

At this point Ivy's eyes began to fill with tears. "Father," she said, "how I wish we could visit the Child and give Him a present. But we have nothing to give Him."

"I'm sure," he told her, "if we had been there, we would have found something." But his attempt to reassure her seemed to fall on deaf ears as she chattered on about the gifts she wished she had to pass on to the child.

Soon her eyelids began to droop, and she started to yawn. Thomas picked her up and laid her on her bed, pulled up the covers, and tucked her in. He stoked the fire, and together they said their prayers. Thomas remained up a little longer until the fire began to die down. He put on another log, and then he, too, climbed into bed, where he lay for some time before he drifted off to sleep.

With the story fresh in her mind, Ivy began to dream. She dreamed Jesus came to her and told her He planned to visit her on Christmas Day. She awoke the next morning when her father came in from the cold with a few more logs for the fire. "Father," she said excitedly, "Jesus is coming to visit us today."

"Really," her father said, barely able to contain his skepticism.

While she put on her clothes, Ivy told him about her dream, and then she joined her father by the fire. After the cottage warmed a bit, Ivy pulled out the treats she had set aside for their Christmas dinner: a loaf of bread as well as a few carrots, some potatoes, and a few seasonings she planned to make into a Christmas stew. To this she added a mincemeat pie, the spiced mixture of dried fruit, cinnamon, cloves, and nutmeg placed in the oval-shaped bowl that represented the crib used by Christ at His birth. She placed the pot on the fire and began to heat the water she needed to prepare the stew.

Two hours later, with the stew simmering on the fire, she set the table. But instead of the two places she normally set at the table, she set a third place, as she told Thomas, "for Jesus."

It was then they heard a knock on the door. Ivy flew to open the door, but instead of Jesus, she instead saw an old man. He stood in the open doorway so cold and stiff he could barely speak. "Would it be possible," he asked, "to warm myself by your fire for a few moments? I won't trouble you long. Once I'm warm, I'll be on my way again."

"Why, of course," Ivy's father said. As he looked at the table set for three, he added, "And would you join us for dinner? We even have a place set at the table for you."

It was difficult for Ivy to hide her disappointment. She had so hoped Jesus would join them for this Christmas dinner. Now she knew their meager rations must be split three ways. Putting on a smile that first seemed forced, she dished up the food.

As the man warmed, she learned his name was John. He had traveled a considerable distance to reach the home of his only son, who had invited him to live with his family. Caught in the storm, he had lost his way and, afraid he might perish in the cold, prayed God would lead him to shelter. Then he saw the light from Thomas's small cottage in the clearing just beyond the forest through which he had come. Had he not come upon their home, he was convinced he would have died.

John, as it turned out, was a wonderful storyteller and kept them entertained into the early afternoon when they heard yet another knock on the door. Again Ivy remembered her dream and rushed to open the door. But instead of Jesus, she found instead a young women holding an infant. More quickly this time, she invited the young mother in, still disappointed her dream seemed destined not to come true. She learned the woman's name was Clara. Thomas asked if she had eaten yet that day, and the woman shook her head no. She told him her husband had died the month before, and after settling her affairs, she had gone to live with a sister in a nearby village. However, that morning, her brother-in-law, concerned about the family's dwindling food supplies, evicted her and the child, whom she called Cilia. So she set out to travel to her brother's home some miles beyond the cottage.

Ivy set a place for her at the table, then put on her coat and went around the back of the cottage to the stable where she milked the goat to add a bit more to her meal. When she arrived back inside, she was surprised to see the woman eating some of the stew she'd prepared that morning. She was certain the bowl had been empty after dinner with John an hour before. So she blinked her eyes and looked again to see Clara dip her spoon into a full bowl of stew and nibble on a piece of the bread Ivy thought was gone.

Once Clara had eaten and had nursed the baby, the four of them gathered around the fire. Clara, as it turned out, had the voice of an angel, and the four of them sang Christmas carols until the late afternoon sun began to fade on the horizon.

As the music ended and the conversation reached a lull, yet again there was a knock on the door. This time it was Thomas who opened the door. Before them was a priest, garbed in his habit, a walking staff in his hand. Brother Nicolas introduced himself. He, too, had seen the light of the cottage in the forest and with daylight fading thought he might find a safe place to warm up before he headed to the priory a few miles beyond the nearby village.

"Of course," Thomas said while Ivy sprang into action. She took her own bowl and spoon and quickly went out to wash them off. She returned, set them on the table, and went to the fire, where she dipped the ladle into the pot and again was astonished to find enough of the stew to make up a full bowl. After this she was only slightly surprised to see her father set down a thick slice of bread beside the friar's bowl as he began to eat his dinner.

The priest apologized for imposing on them. He told them he had underestimated how long it would take traveling through the deep snow. And having veered off course, he knew he'd be unable to reach his destination until the next day.

Thomas had already invited all of their visitors to spend the night. "Just last night," he announced, "my dear Ivy here said she was prepared to give up her bed for the baby Jesus and His parents. I guess we'll have to settle for the likes of you."

After the sun had set, Ivy brought out the mincemeat pie and divided it five ways. Despite what her eyes said, it seemed all of them had somewhat bigger pieces than she saw come out of the bowl. They washed the pie down with surprisingly full mugs of goat's milk. After they had finished, the visitors and Ivy and her father continued to talk until well into the night.

As the talk turned to Christmas, Ivy asked her father to bring out the crèche he had carved in the long, cold winter evenings. The night before, he had finished the last of the figures: the small statue of Mary. When Ivy had held this one in her hands, she was struck by the beauty of the Mary her father had carved. "She's beautiful," she said softly. She looked into her father's face in time to see a tear escape and run down his cheek. She didn't even need to ask. She knew her father had carved from memory an image of her own mother.

Brother Nicolas was speechless as he looked at the small figures. He took each one in his hands and admired the detail Thomas had carefully carved into each of the witnesses of Christ's birth. The guests looked at her father's handiwork and exclaimed how they had yet to see a set of figures this fine anywhere in the land. Ivy arranged them on the table, each one gazing in the direction of the baby Jesus in the manger.

It was late. Baby Cilia was already asleep, and Clara was the first of the adults to retire, joining the baby in Ivy's bed. Then John, citing his age, prepared to climb into her father's bed.

Father Nicolas had already volunteered to sleep on the floor. "I'm used to a stiff bed," he said. "I've slept on worse at the priory." Ivy, Thomas, and Father Nicolas lay down side by side on the floor, their feet by the fire, and covered up with their cloaks to keep warm.

In the moments before Ivy fell asleep, she thought of her dream from the previous evening. She was still disappointed Jesus had not made an appearance. But she was glad for their visitors and marveled how the little she had set aside for the day had gone so far. At an age where the remarkable still seemed more than possible, she believed something important had taken place.

When Ivy woke, her father had once again stoked the fire. The two men helped him set the table. Brother Nicolas had produced a small cake wrapped in a cloth; when combined with some more of the goat's milk, it made a nice breakfast.

Soon each of their visitors would be on their way. It was then Ivy remembered what her father had read to her on Christmas Eve, especially the part about the wise men who brought gifts to Jesus. Suddenly she had an idea. She slipped quietly across the room to her father as he added a log to the fire. She hopped up on a stool and whispered something in his ear. After more than a minute, a smile spread across his face; he nodded, and she stepped down from the stool.

As the three adults bundled up to resume their journeys, Ivy scurried around the room, gathering a few items from various places in the cottage. Then she approached each visitor, handing each one something she had selected specially for that person. To John, she gave a fresh loaf of bread; where it came from she did not know, but it was there, so she took it and put it in his hands. To Clara, she gave a thick woolen cape. It had been her mother's, and her father agreed Clara needed it more than they did. And to Brother Nicolas, she gathered up all the figures from the crèche, which she placed in a folded-up bit of cloth.

"I've kept one," she told him, "but Father will carve you a new Mary and send it to you with the next traveler who goes your way." Ivy was generous, but she couldn't take the risk her father wouldn't get the next Mary quite this perfect.

The storm from the day before had ended. The wind had died down, and the bright sun shone off the white snow and warmed the air. The guests left, each headed in a different direction.

Ivy and her father stepped back into the cottage. "Well," her father said, as he picked her up in his strong arms, "that was quite a Christmas."

"Yes, it was," she agreed. "But Jesus didn't come."

"I think," her father said, "you might be mistaken. I think He did. Just not in the way you expected."

In the weeks that followed, several more remarkable events took place around the cottage. The day the visitors left, Thomas found a small bag of gold coins under his pillow. A week later when Thomas opened the door, they found a satchel containing cheese, sausages, and several hams. Then, in early spring, a stranger arrived leading a cow, which he insisted he was under orders to deliver to Thomas.

Ivy grew to become a beautiful young woman. However, it was her kindness for which she became known. When asked the reason for her sensitive spirit and generous heart, she would simply say, "You never know when Jesus might pay you a visit."

LET'S TALK

1. Listening to her father read the Christmas story, Ivy wanted to make sure the Holy Family had a place to stay and enough to eat. How is this desire tested during the story? How can you serve others in need this Christmas?

2. Ivy had a dream Jesus would visit them on Christmas Day. She even set a place at the table for Him. Though He didn't literally come, why does her father tell her he believes Jesus visited them? When Jesus was an adult (Matthew 25:34–40), He told His disciples that anything they did for others, they were doing for Him. How does this perspective change the way you treat others?

CHRISTMAS REFUGEE

They met in June—two young mothers looking for relief from an early heat wave and the chance to let their five-year-old boys burn off some energy.

It was just after lunch when Jennifer and her son, Caleb, left for the park. They made their way down the three flights of stairs from their small apartment and walked the five blocks to the park. Caleb had on *Star Wars* swim trunks, impatient for the chance to play in the park's wading pool. They moved slowly; Jennifer was eight months' pregnant, and at this point, everything about daily life was uncomfortable. The night before, her husband, Michael, burst out laughing as she tried to cut up a watermelon with a similar-sized bump separating her from the counter. But now the challenge was to make it four more blocks to the park without tripping.

They waited for the light to change, then made their way across the street to Ellis Park. The wading pool was situated just past the playground, and Caleb ran quickly to the gate. "Hurry up, Mom," he said, anxious to get in the water as quickly as possible. Once she opened the gate and applied suntan lotion to his squirming body, he was in, making full use of all eighteen inches of pool water.

Jennifer and Michael had moved to the city in June so he could pursue doctoral studies in biomedical engineering. They knew the next four years would be busy. Classes, lab work, and teaching would occupy most of his time. In the eight weeks since their arrival, Jennifer had met a few moms, but she wasn't anywhere close to replacing the great friends they'd left behind. Caleb especially was feeling the lack of age-appropriate playmates. His mom wasn't nearly as fun as she'd been even just a few months earlier when she could get down on the floor and play LEGOS.

But right now Caleb was just happy to be in the water. "Watch me swim," he said, lying down and pretending to swim on his back. Then Jennifer saw her, standing a dozen feet away, dressed in traditional North African garb, including a hijab. With the temperature already close to 90 degrees and the humidity at 70 percent, she looked hot. But what caught Jennifer's eye was that she was pregnant. In fact, she guessed, it looked as if they were due about the same time.

Jennifer looked back toward the water and noticed Caleb had begun to play with another little boy. The two splashed each other and laughed as they stomped around in the water. Jennifer looked back in the woman's direction, and she was smiling. Jennifer gave her a quick wave, and the two women, a bit embarrassed, turned back to watch their sons playing together in the water. After a couple of minutes, Jennifer decided to take a risk. She turned, walked the short distance, and said simply, "Hi, my name's Jennifer. Is that your son?"

The woman smiled and said, "Yes." Then added her name was Sahra.

"When is your baby due?" Jennifer asked.

"Next month," Sahra said.

"Really! So is mine," said Jennifer.

The next few minutes the two chatted about simple things. Jennifer learned Sahra's son was named Ibrahim, and he was five, just like Caleb. Sahra was born in Africa and moved to the United States when she was seventeen. She met her husband, Ali, a year later, and they were married after a short engagement in a traditional ceremony. Ali, Sahra told her, worked two jobs—driving a taxi during the day and on weekends, and stocking shelves at a small ethnic market at night. "He's a hard worker," she told Jennifer, "and a good man."

In the course of the conversation they learned both boys would be at the same elementary school in the fall. It was an answer to one of Jennifer's prayers—that Caleb would know at least one other boy when he started school in the fall.

In the next couple of weeks, Jennifer saw Sahra a few times. She had an infectious personality. Even with the language and cultural barriers, the two were able to communicate. And the boys loved to play together in the park and the pool.

It was the last day of July when Jennifer felt the contractions. Michael came home quickly from the lab, and they dropped Caleb off with the wife of a coworker, then drove the short distance to the hospital. Twelve hours later Jennifer gave birth to a baby girl, whom they named Lily. Caleb was happy enough when they arrived home two days later. However, he seemed to have expected an instant playmate. Since little Lily didn't do much, he treated her with casual indifference.

At the kindergarten roundup four weeks later, Jennifer saw Sahra again. She, too, had a new baby, also a little girl. "What is her name?" Jennifer asked.

"Ayanna," said Sahra. "It means 'beautiful flower.'"

Jennifer laughed. "My daughter's name means flower as well!" Before they left the school, they agreed to meet the next week at the park with their daughters while the boys were in school.

Jennifer and Sahra continued to meet weekly at the park until the weather turned cold at the end of October. Jennifer suggested they meet the next week after school and walk together with the boys to the local public library.

To the average person at the library that day, the two women couldn't have seemed more different. They had completely different upbringings, spoke different languages, dressed and acted differently, and had different religious convictions.

Yet they shared a common humanity and had remarkably similar lives. They laughed as they talked about raising children, swapped pregnancy and birthing stories, and shared tips on favorite local restaurants. But in the library, Sahra went a bit further. She told Jennifer that most days she was lonely. Her husband worked from dawn to dusk, and what family she had in the area were too busy. Because she didn't have a car, it was difficult for her to get together with the few friends she had. Sahra's words touched Jennifer, not only out of empathy but because she, too, felt alone in this strange new city. As they packed up to leave for home, Jennifer invited Sahra for lunch the next week and was surprised when she readily accepted.

For the next few weeks, they met weekly either at the library or at Jennifer's for lunch. Sahra asked Jennifer about her life. So Jennifer told her about growing up on a farm outside a small midwestern town. She told her how she'd met her husband in a freshman English class; she'd made an A, he a C. Then how fate had placed them in a biology class the next semester with the results nearly flipped—Michael with the A and Jennifer a B, but only because he offered to tutor her through the course.

Their friendship had blossomed into romance, and they were married the summer after their senior year. They then moved to Texas, where Michael took a job with a chemical company and Jennifer taught high school English. By fall, she was pregnant with Caleb. He was born just after the spring term ended. Jennifer taught one more year and then stayed home with Caleb, taking on freelance editing jobs during naps and evenings to bring in extra cash. It was a comfortable life, but they knew Michael needed to go to grad school, so they made the move nearly 1,200 miles north.

As Jennifer shared more about herself, so did Sahra. One day after lunch while their newborns napped, Sahra shared more about her journey to America. She told Jennifer about the brutal civil war fought in her country between rival factions. By the time Sahra was ten, the war was already twenty years old. Hundreds of thousands were killed, including two of her uncles.

One day a cousin came to their home just after dusk. He told her father his name was on a list of those considered disloyal to the ruling faction. Quietly her father directed everyone in the family to gather the bare essentials. Within minutes, they left. They would never go back.

Hungry, thirsty, and scared, they moved along with others toward what they hoped was a safe place—a refugee camp in a neighboring country. For three weeks they walked, traveling ten or more miles a day. When they arrived at the border, they found armed guards on patrol, making it impossible to go farther. Aid workers gave them food and water but told them they couldn't stay long; it simply wasn't safe.

A few days later, a man came to see Sahra's father at night. He told him he could get the family across the border . . . for a fee. The price was high—they would have little left—but they felt they had no choice, and so two days later they crossed the border at night in an old Land Rover. The drive across the desert took five long days.

They arrived at the refugee camp, where more than 100,000 people lived in a space designed to accommodate 25,000. What they found there discouraged them. Conditions were awful, and many of the refugees at the camp had been there for a long time—some as long as twenty years.

Sahra and her family spent the next five years there. It wasn't easy, especially the waiting game, wondering if they would ever be able to leave and go to a new place and begin to build a new life. The hardest day came three years later when her father became ill. It was never quite clear to Sahra what happened, but even with medical care from a foreign doctor, he didn't get better and died two weeks later. She had never felt so alone. Her father had always known just what to do. She trusted him implicitly. But now he was gone. She wasn't sure what to do next.

Sahra's lucky day came two years later when she learned her family had been chosen to come to the United States. The day they arrived, it was 10 degrees. Fortunately, the host family assigned to meet them had warm coats and boots available for everyone to wear.

Along with her mother, younger brother, and sister, she went to live temporarily with an uncle who had already settled in the city. It was a difficult year. She had to learn English, figure out public transportation, find a job, and learn strange customs.

As she listened to Sahra's story, Jennifer couldn't help but be impressed. Sahra had traveled several hundred miles by foot, perhaps a thousand by truck, and another 10,000 miles by plane to come to America. Any hardship Jennifer had experienced paled in comparison to what Sahra had already faced.

Because Michael was busy with graduate school, he told Jennifer they'd travel home for Christmas but needed to stay put Thanksgiving week. So the Saturday after Thanksgiving, Jennifer invited Sahra and her family over for lunch. They said yes. It would be the first time for the husbands to meet.

The only anxiety Jennifer had was that they had already decorated their small apartment for Christmas; Caleb insisted on it. Friday they found a small tree and decorated it with the few ornaments she had collected in their short marriage. Jennifer worried Sahra and Ali would be offended, but they didn't seem to mind when they arrived. Her only concession had been to move the crèche from the coffee table to the top of the dresser in Caleb's bedroom.

Jennifer had cleared the menu in advance, and soon they began to eat and get acquainted. Ali's English was good. He told Michael he had lived in a refugee camp where English was spoken since he was ten.

Caleb and Ibrahim finished their lunch long before the others and disappeared to his room. Sometime later Jennifer realized she didn't hear the boys' voices. Curious, she went to investigate, and what she discovered made her heart skip a beat. There on the floor in Caleb's room were the boys, the figurines from the crèche spread out before them while Caleb told Ibrahim the Christmas story. Concerned not to offend her guests, she said gently, "Caleb, could you put the crèche back where you got it? You and I can play with it later."

"But," Ibrahim said, "I want to hear the rest of the story."

Then Sahra walked up. "Don't worry," Jennifer said. "I've asked the boys to put the figurines up. Caleb can play with them later."

Once she grasped what the boys were up to, Sahra was unconcerned. "It's okay," she said. "We know who Jesus is." Jennifer knew this was only partly true since their respective faiths have a different understanding of Jesus. "Go on," Sahra said to Caleb. "Tell us the story." Jennifer gasped.

Somehow, the conversation from the bedroom attracted the attention of the men, and soon both Michael and Ali were there as well. "Ali," Sahra said, "Caleb is about to tell us the story of Jesus."

"Oh," Ali said, shrugging his shoulders. So the four of them gathered around as the two boys sat on the floor with the cast of characters scattered out before them.

Without skipping a beat, Caleb said, "I'm gonna start again from the beginning."

"Yeah," said Ibrahim enthusiastically. So Caleb launched into the story and recited it from memory, taking a few liberties along the way.

"You see," he said, "a long time ago a king issued a 'key' that everyone in the world needed to be counted. But to be counted they had to go to the town they were from." Turning to Ibrahim, he said, "That means you would have to go back to Africa."

"No, I wouldn't," said Ibrahim. "I was born here!"

"No," said Caleb confidently, "it wasn't about going back to where you were born, but to where your grandpa was from."

"Oh," said Ibrahim.

Then Caleb took the figurine of Mary and placed her on the back of a slightly beat-up donkey. "Here," he said to Ibrahim, "you take Joseph. We're going to walk them on down the road." Then he turned to look up at the adults and said, "So the mean king made them walk a long way—about a thousand miles, I think—to go back to Bethlehem where his grandfather David was from."

The two boys moved the figurines across the floor, under bedposts, and around a lampstand until they brought them to a stop a few feet away from where they had started.

Then Caleb continued: "So Mary," he said, "had a baby in her tummy, and they needed a place to stay. But none of the hotels in town had a room, so they went to stay in a stable."

"Really?" said Ibrahim. "Why didn't they just go to a hospital? That's where my mom went when my sister was born."

"Mine too," said Caleb. "But they didn't have hospitals then, silly. Don't you know anything?" Jennifer gasped again, but Ali just laughed so she relaxed.

By this time, Caleb had moved Mary into the stable and told Ibrahim to move Joseph in right beside her. Then he continued, "That night Mary had a baby. She wrapped him in some rags because she didn't have any diapers and put him in a manger. That's what cows eat hay out of," he added, in case anyone wondered. Then he retrieved the baby Jesus figurine from the pile and put him in the little manger. He told Ibrahim to help him place the animals around the baby. "I think they all waited outside till the baby was born," he said. "It was a little loud in there until Jesus came out," he added. Jennifer was glad he didn't go into any more detail.

Then Caleb grabbed one of the shepherds and handed the other to Ibrahim. "They go there," he said, placing his shepherd a foot or so behind the stable. Then he placed the two sheep in front of the shepherds and told everyone the shepherds were watching their sheep in a field outside of town. "Then," he said, "a big angel came all lit up and told them not to be afraid, but they were and fell down and hid their faces." Then Caleb put his shepherd's face down on the carpet and instructed Ibrahim to do the same.

"Then," Caleb said, "the angel told them to go to town and see the baby Jesus. But before they could go, even more angels showed up and sang a Christmas carol." Then he paused for a second, looked up at Jennifer, and said, "Mom, do you know which one they sang?" She shook her head no, and Caleb turned his attention back to the scene unfolding in front of him.

He took his shepherd, stood him up, and walked him to the front of the stable. Ibrahim followed his lead but then asked, "What did they do with the sheep? They didn't leave them in the field, did they?"

"Nah," said Caleb, "I think they followed the shepherds. That's what sheep are trained to do." The boys moved the sheep up by the shepherds so they could look in on the baby at the center of the scene.

"What about these guys?" Ibrahim asked, pointing to the three wise men.

"They're next," said Caleb. "They didn't come until the next day when the animals went back out into the fields." He moved the animals away from the front of the stable.

Then he told the story of the star. "It was mega bright," he said, holding his hand above the stable.

"What did it look like?" asked Ibrahim.

"I'm not sure," said Caleb. After a pause, he got up quickly and went to his nightstand, where he retrieved a small flashlight. He turned it on and held it above the stable. "Maybe something like this," he said.

Then he went on to tell the story of how the wise men came from a long way off to bring presents to the baby Jesus. "What did they give him?" Ibrahim asked.

"Gold, Frankenstein, and mirrors, I think," he said. Michael let out a laugh, and Jennifer smiled.

"Is that it?" Ibrahim asked, noticing Caleb had now used up all the available actors.

"No," said Caleb. "One more bad thing happened. The king wanted to kill baby Jesus, but another angel—a littler one, I think—came and warned Joseph to go away so the king couldn't find them."

"Where did they go?" asked Ibrahim.

"Egypt," said Caleb.

"That's in Africa!" said Ibrahim excitedly.

"For real?" said Caleb.

"Yes," said Michael. "Ibrahim's right. The family stayed there for a few years until there was a new king and it was safe to go back home."

With the story finished, Caleb and Ibrahim put the crèche back together on top of his dresser. Both sets of parents made their way out of the bedroom, the men heading to the living room and the women to the kitchen.

When Jennifer and Sahra were alone, Sahra said softly, "He was refugee."

"What?" said Jennifer, not quite certain what she'd heard.

"Jesus, He was a refugee too," said Sahra again as tears formed in her eyes.

Jennifer had never thought about it quite that way. But then she remembered what she knew of Sahra's story—how political unrest displaced her family and how they have been separated by a senseless civil war. Then she saw the parallels. Mary and Joseph had to travel to Bethlehem because of the whims of a Roman emperor. Then the entire family had to flee the country because of the jealousy of a king.

"That's right," said Jennifer. "And it wasn't the last sad thing that happened to Him." She hoped one day to have the opportunity to tell her new friend more about Jesus.

By now, the babies were walking up from their naps. Soon it was time for Sahra and her family to leave.

Later that night, with dishes washed and the house picked up, Jennifer sat on the couch and looked at the crèche they'd returned to the center of the coffee table. Sahra's comment continued to reverberate in her mind: "Jesus was a refugee too."

She remembered what she had learned as a child—that Jesus had given up the comforts of heaven for the difficulties of life on earth. That He had lived a life much like ours, experienced our sorrows, and endured our temptations. He'd even been a refugee in Egypt. Jennifer also knew the rest of the story—how years later He was unjustly arrested, tried, mocked, spit upon, condemned, flogged, and crucified, bearing our sin and dying our death because of His great love.

As she thought back to the story Caleb had led them through, she remembered a line he'd left out. It was just after the shepherds returned to their flocks in the field that Mary, amazed by all the shepherds said to her, "treasured up all these things and pondered them in her heart." Jennifer, too, felt amazed; she, too, pondered them in her heart, a heart now full of joy.

LET'S TALK

1. Despite differences in background, language, and religious upbringing, Jennifer and Sahra found that as young mothers, they had much in common. Do you have someone in your life who is different from you? What can you do to find what you have in common rather than focusing on the differences?

2. Sahra's refugee experience was very difficult. What did she find similar between the Christmas story and her own life journey? At the end of the story, what else about Jesus did Jennifer hope one day to share with Sahra? What about Christmas connects directly to the events of Easter?

A (NEW) CHRISTMAS CAROL

The lights dimmed and the crowd grew quiet while the musicians began to make their way onstage. In the center, a slender young man, barely out of his teens, sat down behind the drums. To his left, a middle-aged man with a close-cropped beard held the neck of an upright bass. To his far right was a stocky man with short gray hair, a well-worn Fender Telecaster electric guitar hanging from his shoulder. And to the drummer's immediate right, another slender man sat behind an array of percussion instruments. He exchanged glances with the drummer, and to those who looked even casually, it was clear they were father and son. Also onstage was another young musician seated on a chair behind a pedal steel guitar. To the more observant or simply better informed, it was clear this young man was related to the guitarist.

When all five settled in, a tall, lanky middle-aged but surprisingly fit man began to make his way toward the front of the stage where a high stool sat positioned behind a microphone. The audience began to clap, the volume slowly building as the man sat down and a roadie handed him a well-worn Martin D-28 guitar. A few whistled, and someone from the back yelled out "Jack" while he put the strap over his shoulder, a thin smile on his face as he gazed out at those gathered on a brisk December Sunday night.

✳ ✳ ✳

His longtime agent called the concert "Christmas with Jack," featuring Jack and a few friends and family. It was true, although it hadn't always been that way. Jack and the three middle-aged men onstage were the original members of the '70s rock phenomenon Sonic Boom. Jack played rhythm guitar and sang lead vocals for twenty largely successful years before his ego got the best of him and he left the band to go solo. The other three, onstage together for the first time since 1995, had turned on Jack for his betrayal. Bitter lawsuits and a contentious and public feud spilled out onto the pages of *Spin* and *Rolling Stone*. This went on for the next ten years until calmer heads prevailed, and the four reached a settlement while the lawyers collected their large fees. Few, if any, thought they'd ever see the band on a stage again. Yet here they were, about to perform a concert of Christmas music, a creative decision that seemed incongruous with the band's renegade reputation. A brief blurb in *The New Yorker* questioned if the ad for the concert was a prank and predicted the result could well be the worst Christmas musical event since Bob Dylan's disastrous 2009 Christmas album.

The family part of Jack's agent's promo was about the two young men on the stage, both sons of original members of the band. And later in the concert Amy Simon, wife of Bill, the lead guitarist, would make an appearance on keys. But now it was just the six of them.

✳ ✳ ✳

Jack settled in and turned back toward the twenty-year-old on the drums; when he nodded, Dakota clicked off four beats, and the band roared to life with a spirited rendition of "Santa Claus Is Comin' to Town," complete with sleigh bells. Then without a pause, they transitioned into "Jingle Bells" and brought it down a bit into a swing version of "Winter Wonderland." The audience clapped appreciatively, although it was clear some in the crowd had trouble figuring out exactly what they were hearing. Those who expected to hear '70s and '80s rock arrangements of Christmas carols began to readjust expectations; clearly, this concert was a lot mellower than any Sonic Boom concert they remembered. Jack handed his guitar to a tech, cleared his throat, and thanked everyone for coming. To the hard-core Sonic Boomer, Jack seemed subdued. Known for his frenetic energy and nonstop motion onstage, it was disorienting to see him sitting so calmly on the stool.

Jack's agent, Seymour, selected the Granada, the midtown New York City theatre, as the venue in true Goldilocks fashion. If the juxtaposition of Jack Campbell playing Christmas music was too great, he didn't want to be on the hook for lots of empty seats. But on the other extreme, he did want to make a little money. Jack, to his credit, didn't ask for much in return. As he told Seymour when he mentioned the idea back in June, "I want to make a little music." So here they were—and a mostly full theatre left Seymour satisfied he'd gotten it about right.

"It's been a while," said Jack to the audience, "but we're glad to be here today. This next song features our percussion section. Most of you know Charlie"—he shot a glance at his longtime drummer, tonight on percussion—"but you may not know his kid Dakota back on the kit." Jack's diction betrayed his London roots, even though he'd lived in the States for most of the last thirty years. With this short introduction, Dakota hit his snare drum with the familiar rhythm of "The Little Drummer Boy." Within thirty seconds, everyone knew the concert wasn't slapped together at the last minute. Dakota and Charlie soon competed to outdo one another. Whenever Dakota improvised on the drums, Charlie would match with some inventive use of the dozen or so hand percussion instruments at his disposal. Back and forth it went, the rest of the band joining in, while a smiling Jack sang to keep it moving forward. When the band reached the climax and finished it off, the audience erupted with cheers and applause. Even hard-core Boomers would later admit that while this wasn't what they had expected, it was special.

In his twenty years with Sonic Boom and for most of the next fifteen years since the band broke up, Jack lived out every rock-and-roll cliché. He lived too hard and too fast with little regard for others or himself. Fifteen years earlier he had checked off another box on the list and married the supermodel Brigitte in a private wedding on a beach in the south of France. Brigitte was one of those rare individuals for whom a last name is unnecessary. She was twenty-five at the time and at the top of her game. The wedding itself was more calculated than it seemed. Brigitte was her given name, not one given her by the modeling agency to invoke some exotic appeal. And she was not from France but from Queens, her last name a solidly American "Miller." Her mother had named her Brigitte because she harbored Hollywood dreams for her newborn daughter. For that she'd been partially rewarded. Brigitte had the looks, even if she couldn't act a lick. So modeling it was.

By the time Brigitte and Jack met, they were both tabloid favorites and correspondingly self-centered and emotionally immature. The first five years were up and down, and they almost split up several times until the day Brigitte informed Jack she was pregnant. It stirred something in both of them, and for the beginning of little Charlotte's life, things between them were good. But Jack still hadn't conquered all his demons, and by the time Charlotte turned two, he had begun to act out again. The next six years were rough. There were a few good moments, but only a few. Then came the moment Jack now saw as the beginning of his redemption, although it didn't seem like that at the time. Now, two years later, being here onstage even if no one showed up was, for him, the defining moment in a journey he'd been on since that fateful December day two years ago.

When applause for "The Little Drummer Boy" began to die down, Bill's wife, Amy, an accomplished jazz pianist and singer, slipped onto the stage and took a seat at the piano. Amy slowly began to play "The Christmas Song (Chestnuts Roasting on an Open Fire)." Then on the second time through, she began singing in a sweet, clear voice. Slowly the others, one by one, began to join in, with Jack taking up the harmony. The last time through, Jack invited the audience to sing along. Seamlessly, Amy—along with Tyler, Bill's son, on the pedal steel guitar—began an extended introduction to "The First Noel." A guitar tech wove his way through the band to hand Jack his newly tuned D-28, and he joined in, gently fingerpicking his way into the arrangement. Together the two of them blended in a mellow rendition of the old carol. When they finished, and the muted applause began to die down, Bill began to coax a rowdier sound out of his Tele while the rest joined in on a spirited rendition of "Joy to the World," which morphed into "Feliz Navidad," then a slightly calmer arrangement of "Go Tell It on the Mountain." Jack and Amy finished out the song a cappella.

After the applause died down, Jack took a few moments to introduce a few members of the band, including Danny on upright bass. Then he said, "I know we have only a few young ones here tonight, but these next three songs are for a special young lady here with me tonight." Smiling at a beaming ten-year-old seated on the front row, he led the band in a medley of songs aimed at the younger set—"Frosty the Snowman," followed by "Rudolph the Red-Nosed Reindeer" and "Here Comes Santa

Claus." With plenty of opportunities for a band clearly at the top of its game to shine, the applause at the end was generous.

Then Charlie, Bill, and Tyler exited the stage, leaving Jack, Dakota, Danny, and Amy to finish out the opening set with a moody take on "White Christmas" and a slightly peppier version of "Have Yourself a Merry Little Christmas." With a quick "We'll be right back," Jack and the others made their way offstage for the intermission.

In the green room just off the stage, Jack and the others rehydrated and recouped a bit of energy for the second half. Jack sat pensively fingering the D-28, the guitar handed down to him by his late father. It was a great guitar—just a bit older than Jack himself, so there'd been plenty of time for the wood to open up—and the sound out of the instrument was breathtaking. Jack's dad, Robert, had loved his son, even when, for most of Jack's adolescent and young adult years, he had rebelled against his father. Jack's dad and mom got religion during the Jesus People movement in the late 1960s. They spent their weekends at conferences where Jack's dad would play this guitar and sing "Kumbaya" (literally) while the assembled crowd passed the time between speakers.

Jack had rebelled against the religion, but he caught the music bug. At nineteen, he started playing in a band. Then he met Bill and Danny—and not long after, Charlie—and the four founded The Sonics, which morphed into Sonic Boom when the band saw a television news report about the Concorde supersonic jet. Jack and Bill were the band's primary songwriters. Soon they had a dozen or so original songs to go along with a handful of covers, and they found a following playing at an assortment of London pubs.

About this time, two significant events took place almost simultaneously. First, Jack and his dad had a falling out. Jack's lifestyle choices and his disrespect for family values became more than his father could handle, and his normally mild-mannered father kicked him out of the house. Only a few weeks of crashing at friends' flats passed before a representative for Eureka Records heard the band play at a pub one night and signed them on the spot. An advance helped the band (barely) get by until the first album *Sonic Boom* was released six months later and became an instant hit. The single "Double Shot" went quickly into the top of both the British and American pop charts, and the band was off.

For the next ten years they recorded at a steady pace, about an album a year, and toured at least six months of the year. The second decade together wasn't nearly as productive—just three albums and another one uncompleted when a combination of poor choices and petty squabbles led to a six-month silent breakup. The folks at Eureka got the band together long enough to finish the band's twelfth album, *Ambush*, before the wheels came off. First, the critics bashed the record. Then Jack's immaturity and refusal to take responsibility for his actions led him to decide he didn't need the others. So he took the songs he'd been working on to Boom Alley Records and quickly recorded a solo record that did well. For about five years, Jack's career still had some momentum. But after a while his bad habits and dwindling creative output made it clear he would soon be a has-been. But Jack was stubborn, and it would take nearly a decade for him to get it. Along the way, small pockets of success fueled the delusion he could keep doing what he'd been doing and everything would be okay. The most recent effort was three years ago when he landed a six-month guest appearance on the reality show *Who's Next Up Front?*, a contest to pick a new lead singer for the band Drive Shaft after Charlie Pace went missing in a plane crash somewhere over the Pacific.

The door to the green room opened, and Seymour gave everyone a five-minute warning. The tech handed Jack his guitar, and he got ready to head back out. The plan was to start the second half stripped down and acoustic. With just Jack on guitar, Danny on bass, and Amy on vocals, they began with the American folk carol "I Wonder as I Wander." Then with Jack joining in, the two of them sang "What Child Is This?" with Tyler on pedal steel. Then the rest of the band made their way to the stage for upbeat arrangements of "Hark! The Herald Angels Sing," "O Come, All Ye Faithful," and "Angels We Have Heard on High." Pausing to regroup and tune while the applause died down, Jack looked down at little Charlotte, now ten, seated next to his long-suffering wife. His "angels," as he now called them.

Two years earlier, on a Monday in early December, Jack's cell phone rang. It was his mother. She told him that his father, by then in his mid-seventies, had been diagnosed with stage 4 liver cancer. Over the years Jack visited his parents every year or so when his travels took him to London. The visits were generally short and cordial. The animosity Jack felt toward his dad had long since faded. But each time he was there, he felt uncomfortable. It wasn't because his father said anything judgmental or condemning. In fact, his dad was always gracious. With a few more years and a bit of introspection foreign to his nature, Jack knew the uneasiness came because of the contrast between the way he'd chosen to live his life and the way his father had chosen to live his. Around his father, a selfless man who'd spent his retirement years serving the poor at a crisis center, he felt narcissistic and coarse.

The next day Jack, Brigitte, and Charlotte got on a plane to London. When they arrived, they checked into a hotel Seymour had booked for them not far from the hospital. Then the three of them got in a cab and made the ten-minute journey to see Jack's dad for the first time in a year. When he walked in, Jack could see his dad was in pain. His mother had already told him the doctors said there was nothing they could do but try to make his father comfortable. The next morning, they began administering meds to help him deal with the pain. The plan was to figure out the correct base dosage, then let him go home as long as was possible before his condition worsened.

"Hello, Son," his dad said.

"Dad" was all Jack could get out. Beside him, both Brigitte and Charlotte were in tears. Both gave Jack's dad a hug, and then it was Jack's turn. When they hugged, his father said simply, "I love you."

"I know," said Jack, through tears. He thought of the choices he'd made in the thirty years since he'd abruptly left home. And with blinding clarity, he realized how selfish he'd been—selfish and foolish. Here was a good man. A man who loved him. He knew his father regretted how the two of them had once fought. But he also knew his father's regrets were nothing compared to his own.

The next few days were filled with visits to the hospital. Then they moved his father back home. They had short conversations as often as five times a day between the naps that occupied much of his father's day. Then it came time to leave. Brigitte had work to do at a new design house she had partnered with. And Charlotte needed to get back to school.

The last day they were there, Jack spent most of it in his father's bedroom. His father slept much of the morning, leaving Jack alone with his thoughts. As he sat, he formulated the words he knew he needed to say. When his dad woke up early in the afternoon, Jack fought the tears below the surface and managed to say, "Dad, I'm sorry for the way I've hurt you. Please forgive me. I love you. You are a far better man than I'll ever be." Both men cried for several minutes.

After a few minutes of silence, Jack's dad wiped his eyes and said, "Thank you, Son. I love you too. And even though you may not want to hear it, so does God. I won't preach to you, but some of the answers you're looking for are in what you heard when you were a child."

Jack nodded, in part to please his father but also because he thought his dad might be right. "Son," his father said. "Could you get something out of the closet?" Jack nodded, walked over, and opened the door. "In the back," his dad said. Reaching back, Jack found a guitar case standing upright in the corner. "I want you to have it."

Jack had spent tens of thousands of dollars on guitars during his career. He'd even broken guitars worth two grand on stage at concerts just for show. Any guitar he could ever want was well within his ability to purchase. But he knew this guitar was and would remain priceless.

Before they left the next morning, before they said their final goodbyes, Jack's mother pulled him into the kitchen. She thanked him for coming and for the time he'd spent with his dad. "Jack," she said, "I hope you don't take this wrong, but I think you need to listen to your wife. There's something different about her, and I think you need to pay attention." Clutching the handle of the guitar case, the three of them slid into the cab that took them to the airport. Jack had called the night before and purchased an extra ticket just for the guitar. He wasn't about to trust the baggage gorillas with this instrument.

Jack looked back out at the crowd, then turned to the band, counted out "one, two, three four," and began singing "O Little Town of Bethlehem." Then they transitioned into "O Come, O Come, Emmanuel." As the last notes rang out and the audience applauded, the musicians, all except Jack, made their way off the stage. Jack adjusted the capo on his guitar and said, "I'd like to sing you a new song. It doesn't yet have a title, so for now we'll simply call it 'A (New) Christmas Carol.'"

Less than forty-eight hours after Jack, Brigitte, and Charlotte got back to New York, Jack got the call from his mom that his dad had passed away. Jack knew he needed to make some changes, but he didn't quite know where to turn. With his mother's voice echoing in his ears, he began watching Brigitte. When his mother had said there was something different about her, he knew she was right. In the last year she'd begun to attend a church on the Upper West Side. She and Charlotte attended every Sunday, and even though they invited him, he always declined. But the first Sunday back, he said yes. Nothing earth-shattering happened, but it made him feel good. The following Wednesday was Christmas Eve. Again he accepted the invitation to go to church. The minister talked about a song St. Luke had included in his description of the birth of Jesus. It was a song sung by an angel choir to a group of shepherds stuck out in a field on a cold night. For all sorts of reasons, shepherds, the minister said, were low-class people in the first-century world. But it was to shepherds that an angel first announced, "I bring you good news that will cause great joy for all the people. Today in the town of David a Savior has been born to you; he is the Messiah, the Lord." Then a choir of angels began to sing: "Glory to God in the highest heaven, and on earth peace to those on whom his favor rests."

Jack had a sense that it was this peace his dad's life had pointed to. He realized what his wife was experiencing was more than a change in lifestyle; she and Charlotte had found the peace he'd always wanted but had looked for in all the wrong places. The minister said the word *angel* means "messenger." In the next six months Brigitte and Charlotte were invaluable guides as Jack struggled to make sense of the message he needed to hear.

Since returning from England, Jack and Charlotte began a new tradition. Every evening after dinner Jack would pull out his father's old Martin, and he and Charlotte would sing. She had a surprisingly good voice. Now here, in front of a few hundred gathered to hear Jack Campbell, former lead singer of Sonic Boom, sing Christmas carols, he motioned for the little girl seated on the front row to join him onstage. A stagehand quickly brought out another stool and microphone. Charlotte wiggled her way onto the stool and smiled at her dad, who began to play the old Martin D-28. Jack began:

On a rocky hill nearby
Watching sheep there abide
A light so bright lit the sky
They were terrified

The glory of the Lord lit the night
Words rang out with delight
Fear not, hear news of cheer
God in heaven is now here
Peace to all tonight
Peace to all tonight

Then Charlotte took over for the second verse:

In a stable not too far
Right beneath a bright star
Lay the one that all adore
Jesus Christ the Lord

Then Jack joined in on the chorus:

The glory of the Lord lit the night
Words rang out with delight
Fear not, hear news of cheer
God in heaven is now here
Peace to all tonight
Peace to all tonight

Together they sang the third and fourth verses—Charlotte with the melody and Jack on harmony.

Once the angels were gone
To a man they were drawn
Was what they heard true?
Mother and child in view

Amazed at what they saw
Spread the news to all
A Savior's been born today
Left them all in awe

Then they sang the chorus one last time:

The glory of the Lord lit the night
Words rang out with delight
Fear not, hear news of cheer
God in heaven is now here
Peace to all tonight
Peace to all tonight

When they had finished, the audience erupted. First a few in the back and then some in the middle and finally everyone in the hall was on their feet. Jack nodded appreciatively, then looked to the front row, where his mother whispered something in Brigitte's ear. Later she told Jack she was afraid that after such a successful debut, Charlotte would forever be hooked on performing.

Charlotte made her way back to her seat, and Jack left the stage—but the cheers continued. Then came the cry "encore, encore." Suddenly Charlotte appeared backstage. She whispered something in Jack's ear, and he smiled. After a brief word to the band, they made their way back onstage. Picking up his dad's guitar one more time, he announced, "We have one more song, but we need your help. I think most of you know it, at least the first verse. We'd love to have you sing with us." Then Jack began to pick out the familiar notes of Franz Gruber's brilliant carol.

Silent night, holy night
All is calm, all is bright
Round yon virgin, mother and child
Holy infant so tender and mild
Sleep in heavenly peace
Sleep in heavenly peace

"Good night," said Jack. "Merry Christmas." Then, one by one, the band left the stage, and everyone in the hall, even the hard-core Boomers, was speechless.

LET'S TALK

1. Jack Campbell's fans had difficulty adjusting their expectations for the sort of concert he and his old band had put together. How did the concert demonstrate Jack had grown up? Why do you think the audience was so quickly won over by something they didn't at first expect?

2. Jack's life began to change when he learned his father had cancer. What did his parents do to reconcile with him? How did his wife, Brigitte, and daughter, Charlotte, help him on his spiritual journey? Is there someone you can encourage on their spiritual journey?

A LITTLE CHRISTMAS MIRACLE

When I was twelve, I saw a miracle on Christmas Eve. That was sixteen years ago, and I believe I'm the only one who saw it—that is, except for the two it happened to. Dozens could have witnessed it if they had only been looking. But I imagine that's the way it is with most miracles—even the recipient may be unaware. In this case the confusion of the moment hid what happened, and I think it's the way God wanted it. But, rather uncharacteristically, I paid attention and knew what I saw was special. I also had the good sense—though I don't know how—to realize that telling anyone would have spoiled the moment. So I haven't said anything in all these years, although I think my Aunt Sonja suspects something. There's always been a knowing way between us.

I'm descended from Scandinavians who immigrated to the upper Midwest in the 1880s. My grandfather's family was Swedish and my grandmother's Norwegian. The joke was theirs was a mixed marriage, but all I ever saw were pictures of blonde, blue-eyed babies. My father was in the middle between an older sister who did everything right and a younger one who did everything wrong. When I was growing up, even though I knew I shouldn't, I liked the one who did everything wrong best.

Katherine, never Kate, was the achiever in the family. Valedictorian of her high school class and voted most likely to succeed, she went off to an exclusive New England college and graduated with honors. After law school she married an equally insecure, overachieving, and humorless man. After a couple of years at a big law firm, they took jobs in the city just an hour from us. Demanding jobs they took far too seriously meant we seldom saw them except on major holidays. Then they'd blow into town for twenty-four hours, only to leave the following day to catch a flight to some tony resort to ski or sit on the beach. Frankly, I was never sorry to see them go.

Aunt Sonja was a freshman in college the year I was born. It was her second shot at college. Three years before, she had tried it the way everyone else did—right after high school—but she quickly became distracted and didn't even finish the fall semester. The second time around went much better, at least for a couple of years. She won a writing award her freshman year and made the honor roll for four straight semesters. Then history repeated itself; she met a guy, they moved in together, and it went south from there. A couple years later he left, so Aunt Sonja worked odd jobs as a waitress and a clerk in a bookshop and wrote freelance articles for airline magazines to make ends meet.

When I was six, my parents bought a house two blocks from Aunt Sonja's small apartment. My father was largely overlooked in the midst of the family drama, but his virtue as the middle child was an ability to get along with anyone, especially Sonja. My mother, with dark hair and a German-sounding last name, was always ill at ease with my grandparents. It's one reason she showed Sonja so much kindness. Although I didn't know it at the time, Sonja's life was out of control most of the time. She'd surface at our house for a meal every week or so and, on occasion, invite me to her place to read books. It was never neat and tidy, and I saw items like beer bottles that I never saw at Grandma and Grandpa's. But I liked her. She'd tell me, "Now, Peter, make sure you study hard and stay out of trouble." It wasn't until much later that the irony of her advice registered at all.

By the time of the miracle, Sonja and my grandparents had reached an uneasy truce. They were cordial to one another, but the awkwardness was palpable even to a twelve-year-old.

Grandma treated me kindly and indulged me in many ways. I was her only grandchild. Katherine and her dour husband seemed too busy for children, and my mother almost died when I was born, so the doctor suggested they not try for a second. Grandma fussed over me. She always had cookies ready in the cookie jar when I came and took an interest in my life. Grandpa and I talked sports, and he'd take me to ball games where he'd buy whatever I wanted to eat. I liked my grandparents, and I think they were pleased with me. But the sadness that I was their only grandchild was profound.

I was far from a perfect child. It was mostly harmless mischief, and I seldom got caught. I was most rebellious about things I didn't see the purpose in, like church Christmas pageants. When I was seven or eight, it was fun to hang out in my bathrobe with a towel tied around my head, but by the time I was twelve, it was the last thing I wanted to do.

Mrs. Anderson, it was rumored, had been the director of the Christmas pageant since the late 1890s. She'd written the script, which she treated like Holy Scripture; directed the music; and sewed the costumes, which, I believe, were last replaced in the late 1950s. In early November, she'd cast the play. The older girls wanted to be Mary, and the guys, wise men; there were only three of them, and the robes were way cooler than the shepherds'. She liked her innkeepers a bit on the menacing side, so she always chose the biggest boy to be the innkeeper. The younger girls were angels, and the younger boys were shepherds. These parts were infinitely elastic—you can never have too many angels and shepherds.

That year I asked if I could be the donkey, and a few of the guys snickered. We all knew there weren't any animals in Mrs. Anderson's pageants. A few years earlier, when numbers were up in the first- and second-grade class, she had a few of the boys impersonate sheep. They took their parts seriously but could never quite get down when they were supposed to bleat. And one of them forgot what sound sheep make and let out a terrific howl that had the three kings in hysterics.

After handing out a few more of the minor parts, she turned to me and, with utter sincerity, told me I would have the privilege of being Joseph. I briefly protested, but it was clear she'd made up her mind. And if it wasn't bad enough, she then asked Sara Lundgren to be Mary. "Quiet, children!" she snapped as a roar went up from the back row. I slumped in my chair while the rest of the guys gave me the business. Mrs. Anderson handed us our scripts, along with the rehearsal schedule, and instructed us to memorize our lines. On the way out of class, I quietly dropped the script and schedule in the trash.

The first rehearsal took place on the Saturday after Thanksgiving. At 9:30 a.m., the phone rang at our house. It was Mrs. Anderson asking my mother where I was. I got an earful in the car on the way to church. When I arrived, Mrs. Anderson was instructing a group of fidgety shepherds how to kneel before the baby Jesus. Then she turned and informed me, in a low but firm voice, that due to my irresponsibility, Kenny Patterson now had the privilege of being Joseph. Kenny shot me daggers from the center of the platform, where he stood arm in arm with Sara Lundgren, while I took my place on the back row with the rest of the kings. Someone handed me a cigar box covered with silver wrapping paper and filled with pretend frankincense, and we bumbled our way through the rest of the rehearsal.

Later in the week Aunt Sonja came for dinner. After Christmas cookies and hot chocolate, I cleared the table while Aunt Sonja and Dad did the dishes, and then I worked on homework. I was a bit surprised she didn't leave then, but she chatted with my mom in the living room while Dad helped me with some math, and then she stepped in to help me finish an essay on the Gettysburg Address. And she was still around when I got ready for bed.

We lived in an old house, and sound traveled easily through the ductwork. My bedroom was over the living room, and if the furnace wasn't running, I could hear most of the conversation in the room below through the vent. That evening I had a sixth sense something was up, so after Mom left the room, I crawled quietly out of bed and across the floor and put my ear to the vent to listen.

I knew then I wasn't supposed to listen in, but if I hadn't, I wouldn't have recognized the miracle when it happened. Over a cup of decaf, Aunt Sonja told my parents she was pregnant. She quickly addressed the question on my mind and told them never to ask who the father was. Then she informed them she planned to raise the baby. She was due, she told them, on the fourth of July. I don't think my parents quite knew how to respond, but after a short pause, I heard my mother say, "That's wonderful, Sonja." My dad is an emotional sap, and it sounded like he got up and gave her a hug. I could hear muffled sobs, and for a few minutes, no one said a word.

Then Sonja told my parents she knew she needed more money coming in and was already trying to secure more freelance writing jobs. She planned to keep her apartment and asked my dad if he could help her fix it up to make it more comfortable for a family. Then my dad asked the other lingering question: "Have you told Mom yet?"

"No," she said. "It might just kill her." I was surprised by the compassion I heard in Aunt Sonja's voice. It never occurred to me that she cared what my grandmother thought about anything she did. I knew of my grandmother's deep disappointment that she hadn't reached her potential or lived by the values she'd been taught as a young girl. But I now realized she hadn't intended to hurt her mom. She was as confused as we were why she did what she did. Now, after all these years, she was worried how her mom would react. She might be happy-go-lucky on the outside, but inside she was still a little girl hoping her mother was pleased with her.

I heard Aunt Sonja's muffled sobs and my mother's comforting words. "It will be okay," she said. "We love you, Sonja. We're here for you. Whatever you need, just let us know."

"I know," she said. "Thanks." For some reason, even as a twelve-year-old, I knew I'd just listened to a holy moment. I wanted to run down and hug Aunt Sonja and tell her I loved her too. I wanted to tell her I would do anything I could for her baby. I'd been let in on a secret I wasn't supposed to know, and it made me feel special. I crawled slowly back into bed, pulled up the covers, and went to sleep wondering if it'd be a boy or a girl. For some reason it didn't matter.

Aunt Sonja told my grandmother the news later in the week. It didn't go well. She told my parents Grandma had cried and said some unkind things about children without fathers. When Aunt Sonja left, Grandpa walked her to her car, telling her eventually everything would be okay; it always took her mother a little time to get used to unexpected news.

The next day my parents told me. I had to act surprised, but I almost slipped up when I told them I knew Aunt Sonja would be a great mom. What I didn't say is I also knew I would be a great cousin.

Three weeks later we had a picture-perfect Christmas Eve. It snowed eight inches on the 23rd, and everything was covered with a beautiful blanket of white. The church was nearly full with just a few empty seats in the back when the service started. Mrs. Anderson always had the kings start at the back of the sanctuary and come in toward the end of the performance while the congregation sang "We Three Kings." That's how I knew my Aunt Sonja slipped in just as the pageant started while the congregation sang "O Little Town of Bethlehem." It's also how I knew my grandmother looked around, just as Sonja took her seat, but turned back quickly so Sonja didn't see her. But I saw the scowl on her face.

The lights dimmed, and the pageant got underway while we went through our well-rehearsed motions. Other than a shepherd who tripped on his robe, the assembled throng onstage was reasonably orderly. Kenny Patterson sat on the hay bale behind the manger with his arm around Sara Lundgren, looking like he was afraid his arm was about to fall off from a massive bacterial infection. Never in my life had I been so rewarded for disobedience.

Pastor Almqvist began his sermon, pointing out the humble circumstances of Jesus's birth. "It took place," he said, "in a crude stable, not in a warm church. The shepherds had smelly robes, not freshly laundered bathrobes. There were noisy animals, not a quiet sanctuary. And Jesus was placed in a feeding trough, not a bassinet."

He went on: Jesus's arrival on Christmas Day was a demotion; He started out in heaven, a place of unimaginable beauty, but came to earth where the first thing He smelled was manure. The Son of God, who lived in sublime fellowship with the Father and the Holy Spirit, became a human being who would, among other things, get hungry and thirsty and tired. From then on He would live not as a king, the one angels bowed down to and worshipped, but as a humble servant, misunderstood and abused by those who should have known better. Eventually, he said, Jesus would die on a cross, the most torturous and awful form of execution possible.

None of this, the pastor said, was a surprise. Jesus knew what He was getting into, but He did it anyway. Why? Because He loved us. There's nothing we can ever do to make God love us any more. In fact, He did what He did, not because He was annoyed with us for messing things up but out of love for us.

What Pastor Almqvist said made sense. I understood that trying to be good to earn God's favor wasn't the point. Instead, we were already accepted because of what Jesus had done. His words made me just a little ashamed I had made Kenny Patterson be Joseph. If Jesus was willing to die for me, surely I could sit there with my arm around Sara Lundgren.

Pastor Almqvist concluded his sermon with a story about a little girl who'd never heard about the baby Jesus. When she heard the hotel didn't have room for Mary and Joseph and the baby had to be born in a barn, she was ticked. She demanded the teacher go find a lawyer and sue somebody. Even after the teacher told her it was okay, that it had happened a long time ago, she wasn't entirely pacified. She also didn't like His name. She didn't know anyone named Jesus and was worried other kids would make fun of Him if He didn't have a normal name like Carl or Jonathan.

The organist began the introduction to "Away in a Manger." Kenny and Sara stood up. Sara reached down and took the baby in her arms. In our church it's traditional for the baby boy born closest to Christmas to be Jesus in the pageant. Mrs. Anderson likes her babies to be about three months old; they're not so small the girls will damage them, but they're still easy enough to pick up and calm if they cry. Unfortunately, that year there'd been a baby drought, so Jesus was Susanna Larson's six-month-old brother. He'd been asleep until the organ cranked up, but now he was awake and hungry and began to scream at the top of his lungs. At first it was amusing, but Sara stood there frozen; she had no idea what to do. At the same time, one of the shepherds got light-headed and crashed into a couple of the smaller shepherds in front of him. And one of the angels, who'd done a little pre-pageant nibbling on the Birthday Party for Jesus cake in the fellowship hall, turned green and well . . . I don't have to tell you what happened next.

It was then the miracle happened. The miracle wasn't that Kenny Patterson had the presence of mind to take the squawking baby from Sara's arms and take him to his mother. It was when, four rows from the back on the right, my Grandma Grace lived up to her name. From where I stood in the front, I saw her slide down the row to the side aisle and make her way to the back of the sanctuary. And then, without anyone noticing, she slipped in beside Sonja and took her hand. From where I was, I saw the two of them, with tears in their eyes, locked in an embrace. Grandma was wise enough not to push anything and didn't resist when Aunt Sonja put on her coat and slid out the back of the church.

In the weeks that followed, Sonja's pregnancy was the talk of the town. To her credit, Grandma Grace quickly put a stop to anyone who tried to console her. "The past may not be what it should have been," she'd say, "but this family sticks together."

That was my last year in the pageant. At thirteen, I could comfortably sit in the pews and watch a whole new crop of unsuspecting bathrobe-clad kids go through the familiar motions as they acted out the ancient tableau. While Mrs. Anderson first refused, Grandma gave her a talking-to, and the next year the baby Jesus was Aunt Sonja's six-month-old baby boy. Halfway through Pastor Almqvist's sermon, he began to cry and had to be taken out. It seemed fitting since it was, after all, Sonja's baby. And Grandma Grace stood there with tears of joy streaming down her face.

LET'S TALK

1. Early in the story we learn that Sonja and her mother have a difficult relationship. Then it gets more difficult. What allows them to get past their difficulties? Why does Peter believe he saw a miracle?

2. Pastor Almqvist said that Jesus's humble beginnings later led to tragedy. Yet, he said, this was not a surprise; Jesus knew what He was getting into. Why was Jesus willing to do this? Why is it so important that after His death, Jesus rose from the dead?

HOME FOR CHRISTMAS

"Happy Birthday, Mom," said the voice on the other end of the phone.

"Thank you, dear," she said.

"If it's okay, we'll pick you up at three. I hope it's not too early. David's concerned about finding seats after the size of the crowd last year."

"That would be fine," said Annaliese Jaeger. She looked forward to the warm sanctuary, decorated with trees, lights, garland, and candles, and the murmur of voices filling the room with excitement. She hung up and tried to remember what she'd been doing before the phone rang. The ding of a timer in the kitchen and the faint smell of molasses escaping from the oven reminded her of the gingerbread men she was baking for the littlest ones to decorate on Christmas Day. Anna had become more forgetful the last couple of years, but between her and Martin, one of them had always remembered whatever the other one forgot. But now he was gone.

Over and over she had played out the scene of his fall on the icy steps outside their front door last February. The broken hip unleashed an avalanche of health issues that ultimately took Martin's life in July. Now, five months later, she was well into a series of firsts and lasts—first

Thanksgiving alone, first time to bake just the Christmas cookies she liked (she skipped the fudge Martin liked so much because she viewed it as a poor imitation of the milk chocolate of her native Austria). And the lasts—the last time she'd exchange cookies with Martha and Barbara, her neighbors for over forty years, and the last time she'd host her own family for Christmas, a tradition since Truman was in the White House.

After this first Christmas without Martin, Anna was moving to an efficiency apartment in the senior center just a few miles away. She knew it was the right decision. Even before Martin's illness, they had planned to make a similar transition the next year. Still, the finality of it all was difficult.

As Anna placed the gingerbread cookies on a cooling rack, she remembered watching her own mother bake in the small, cramped kitchen in their home outside Salzburg.

Anna arrived in America at age fourteen. While fluency in her native German had faded, she had also never quite mastered the casual American accent that came so easily for her younger siblings. Martin used to joke she sounded sophisticated, like Henry Kissinger. But as charming as he found her way of speech, it was a burden to be a teenager with a German accent during the war years. Martin's own family had emigrated from Germany in the 1890s but quickly left their heritage behind. He never had the need or motivation to learn more than a few German words used at family gatherings. When, at sixteen, he brought the beautiful Annaliese to a Jaeger family dinner, her ability to easily converse in German with his grandparents made her an instant hit. Now, almost seventy years later, many still found her accent quaint. Those who inquired inevitably asked whether she'd known the von Trapp family when she lived in Salzburg. "No," she'd say, explaining that the Hofers were working class and never crossed paths with the aristocratic von Trapps.

With the cookies cooling on the rack and the breakfast dishes washed, dried, and put away, Anna went into the living room to the armchair Martin had bought her in 1968, the year Robert, her youngest, had gone away to college. It had been reupholstered twice, each time to update the color and fabric to match the times. But underneath, it was the same comfortable, classic wingback chair in which she had spent part of each day for forty-two years. She picked up a well-worn Bible and opened to Luke 2. There she read the familiar words, "In those days Caesar Augustus issued a decree that a census should be taken of the entire Roman world. . . . And everyone went to their own town to register. So Joseph also went up from the town of Nazareth in Galilee to Judea, to Bethlehem the town of David, because he belonged to the house and line of David."

Anna identified with Mary. She once heard Mary had been no more than fourteen when the events in the story took place. Anna recalled her own journey at a similar age.

She, too, had traveled reluctantly. She'd been comfortable in Salzburg, a beautiful place on the northern boundary of the Alps. It was the birthplace of Wolfgang Amadeus Mozart, and her memories were of a place filled with music. At fourteen, Anna could see the future before her. She would marry, hopefully well, have a family, and live out her days in Salzburg in much the same middle-class manner of her parents and grandparents before her. But her father was a restless sort. In later years, most assumed he had the incredible foresight to see the trajectory of geopolitical affairs, leaving Austria six months in advance of Hitler's annexation. But that wasn't the case. Frustrated by the economic depression and social stratification that put a lid on his ambitions, he had decided to join an uncle who had left Austria in the late 1920s to work in the haberdashery trade in central Illinois. In the teeth of the Great Depression, his uncle had been shrewd enough to buy out the owner of the struggling business for pennies on the dollar. When the Hofers arrived in 1938, they discovered her father had an eye for style in addition to skill with a needle and thread. This, combined with the uncle's savvy business sense, allowed the two of them to grow a successful store even as their competitors struggled in the rationing environment of the war years.

The next four years were hard ones for Anna. She struggled to learn English; the schools provided little in the way of assistance. At first, she'd been a novelty; her cute blonde curls and lilting voice attracted attention. But as Hitler's ominous actions unfolded, suspicion increased. Martin, however, had been smitten from day one. Within a year he had worked up the courage to talk to the shy anxious Annaliese. His extroverted, even brash manner at first turned her off, but eventually she warmed to his attention. By the next summer he found excuses to drop by the store where Anna worked hemming trousers and altering suit coats. Then one July weekend, he asked her to a Saturday night dance. Soon they were seeing each other regularly.

Anna, snapped back from almost seventy years of memories and looked back at the page in front of her. "Joseph went there," the text said, "to register with Mary, who was pledged to be married to him."

Like Mary, Anna's own adolescence had been altered by geopolitics. In her last year of high school, she and Martin began to talk about the future. Thoroughly in love, they hoped to marry as soon as they could. Anna's parents asked her to wait. As soon as he graduated, Martin would have to report to boot camp. But Anna knew it was not just her age and the impending separation that made her parents reluctant. Frankly, they hoped having Martin in Europe or the Pacific would cool down adolescent passions. Martin's family was not well regarded in the community; instead, they were considered hotheads and drunks. The family farm teetered on the brink throughout the Great Depression, and even increased demand for farm products brought on by the War Department's needs had not helped them as it had others in the area.

In April, with most men in the community already in the service, the local draft board decided to defer the conscription of farm boys like Martin until the end of the summer to allow them to harvest their crops. When he learned this, Martin made one final appeal to Anna's father to allow them to marry after their high school graduation, but he refused. In a moment of foolish passion, Anna stormed out of the house with Martin, not to return until after midnight to the apartment the family occupied over the store.

A month later Anna began feeling ill each morning. In June, her mother confronted her. Amidst tears and angry words, Anna admitted she was pregnant. Just seventeen, Anna and Martin were married on July 17, 1943. Anna's father and uncle cleaned out a room for them in the back of the store, and the couple lived there together until September when Martin boarded a train bound for Texas for his twelve weeks of basic training. In early December 1943, he made a brief visit home to see his pregnant wife and then, after a cross-country train ride, got on a ship with 1,000 other fresh recruits bound for the European theater.

Anna's eyes drifted back to the page in front of her. "While they were there," the text said, "the time came for the baby to be born, and she gave birth to her firstborn, a son. She wrapped him in cloths and placed him in a manger, because there was no guest room available for them."

❄ ❄ ❄

On January 13, 1944, Anna gave birth to a son and named him Markus, after a beloved grandfather back in Salzburg. Nine days later, on January 22, 1944, Martin landed as part of the American Fifth Army on a beach near the Italian resort town of Anzio, thirty miles south of Rome. They caught the Germans completely by surprise and moved rapidly inland, achieving their objective in a few short hours. But as Anna would learn from news reports in the weeks that followed, ultimate success would come at a high price. Finally, on June 5, 1944, news came that American troops had liberated Rome. Anna remembered how relieved she felt at the news.

Martin and many in his company remained in Europe until after the war. Anna grew anxious as she anticipated his return. From his letters, he seemed different. He was more serious and mature, yet he had an edge, critical of officers and army life. Finally, word came that he was on his way home. And in October of 1945 Martin saw his son for the first time. The first few months he was back were awkward. After nearly two years apart, and with the added pressure of a child demanding their constant attention, it took time to adjust to their new life.

In January of 1946 Martin got a job at a new factory in town that made automated washing machines, a product whose production had been suspended in the war years. He quickly demonstrated technical competence and an ability to manage people, and he advanced rapidly. By the time Christina was born, they had rented a house in town. Then, with the arrival of Robert in 1950, they bought their first home. The next few years were a blur. Despite Martin's quick advancement at the plant, Anna never quite felt accepted in the local social scene. Her Austrian heritage and the social stigma associated with the way their marriage began contributed to it. Martin didn't care because he had grown up as an outsider, but for Annaliese, it was always hard.

❄ ❄ ❄

Her thoughts returned, and she read on: "And there were shepherds living out in the fields nearby, keeping watch over their flocks at night." Anna looked up in the direction of the fireplace. Slowly she got up from her chair and walked to the open hearth. She picked up a shepherd off the mantle, carefully dusted him, and placed him behind the wise men kneeling before the manger. She sighed and wondered what she'd do with the crèche after she moved. Martin had worked on the hand-carved pieces gradually in the first few years of their marriage until, by the time Robert was born, they had all eleven. Although the colors had faded from more than sixty years of fingerprints, it had always given her husband great pleasure to watch the impromptu pageants as the little ones manipulated the figurines around the stable her own father had handcrafted out of wood the year Markus was born.

Her eyes had misted over this last Thanksgiving weekend when she took the pieces out of the tissue paper that protected the sacred actors eleven months of the year and positioned them in their customary places. Martin had always been the one to unwrap the Holy Family and their companions. The only change she'd made this year was to put them on the mantle instead of on the coffee table as her husband had preferred. He'd wanted them down where the children could play with them, but she'd always been afraid they'd get broken. And she'd been right. Look closely enough and you could see the discoloration where superglue reconnected an angel's wing and a carefully carved replacement horn for the ox that was positioned to the side, surveying the scene. She knew the next morning someone, probably her youngest granddaughter Suzanne, would quickly clear space on the coffee table and bring the set down where the young ones could repeat the ritual three children and seven grandchildren had established before them.

She returned to the chair and again picked up the worn, black leather

Bible. The story continued, describing the shepherds' experience that first Christmas. "An angel of the Lord appeared to them, and the glory of the Lord shone around them, and they were terrified. But the angel said to them, 'Do not be afraid. I bring you good news that will cause great joy for all the people.'"

In the summer of 1953, nine-year-old Markus became ill. It was soon clear he had polio. Wide distribution of a vaccine was still several years away, and Anna recalled the agony of wondering what effect this would have on her son's life. During the crisis, Martha, a neighbor with children similar in age to her own, invited her to a special prayer service at a church in town. Anna went and was moved by the power and sensitivity of those gathered to pray for a wide variety of needs including Markus's. Soon the family began to attend Sunday services. The paralysis Markus first experienced disappeared in a few months and left him with an interest in medicine, so they weren't surprised when he later decided to become a doctor. Eventually the church became a central part of their lives. At first, Martin was reluctant to go, but over time he was as enthusiastic as the rest about this new community. Soon, instead of vague notions about an impersonal God, they were each drawn into a deeply personal relationship with Jesus.

The words of Luke drew her back to the page: "Today in the town of David a Savior has been born to you; he is the Messiah, the Lord. This will be a sign to you: You will find a baby wrapped in cloths and lying in a manger."

❄ ❄ ❄

Soon they had settled into a comfortable rhythm: work, school, church, music lessons, sports. It was 1959 when they bought the house on Innsbruck Lane. They'd been cramped in a small three-bedroom bungalow, where the boys shared a room in the half-story upstairs. But even with twice the space, the house quickly filled up with furniture and the energy of three children and their friends. Then gradually, as each child went away to college, the house emptied until it was just Anna and Martin. When Martin retired as plant manager in 1988, they thought they'd sell the house and find something smaller, but the place was so comfortable and full of memories that they stayed.

❄ ❄ ❄

The ring of a phone broke the spell. She made her way across the room and picked it up. "Hello."

"Grandma, it's Suzanne. Mom told me she's planning to pick you up at three, but Ella asked if she can see you now. Is it okay if we come by a bit early?"

"Yes, of course," Anna answered. Suzanne was her youngest granddaughter, herself now a mother of two: Ella, five, and Jacob, two. Ella was especially fond of her great-grandmother, and the two had developed a special bond. Suzanne offered to bring lunch, and the three of them arrived a half hour later.

Over chicken noodle soup and oyster crackers, Anna listened to Ella's news about kindergarten and what she hoped to get for Christmas. After they put Jacob down for a nap, Anna read to Ella from some of the Christmas books she brought out this time of year. Ella's favorite was a story about the youngest in a family of rabbits who receives a present he fails at first to fully appreciate, only later to see how special it actually is.

At 2:45 p.m. Suzanne left with her two in tow to run home to get them dressed for the service. Christina arrived right at three to pick up her mother for the service. They found seats near the front of the church, and Anna took in the scene, listening to the brass choir play from the balcony. The people filing in filled the room with energy. Then the organist began to play, and the choir joined in singing, "Hark! The herald angels sing, glory to the newborn King." It reminded Anna of Luke's account: "Suddenly a great company of the heavenly host appeared with the angel, praising God and saying, 'Glory to God in the highest heaven, and on earth peace to those on whom his favor rests.'" A warm glow settled on her as she joined in with the congregation: "Peace on earth and mercy mild, God and sinners reconciled."

After the service she joined Christina and her family for a Christmas Eve dinner and a birthday cake with the number 86 etched in frosting on the top. At 8:30 p.m. Anna asked Suzanne to take her home before it got too late. The house was quiet when she walked in. The next day when the family gathered, it would be a different scene. She made a cup of peppermint tea. Back in the living room she sat down, took the open Bible from the end table, and read, "So they hurried off and found Mary and Joseph, and the baby, who was lying in the manger. When they had seen him, they spread the word concerning what had been told them about this child, and all who heard it were amazed at what the shepherds said to them."

Annaliese Jaeger, too, was amazed as she looked around the room and recalled so many memories. She thought back to the frightened young girl who arrived in this midwestern town seventy-two years earlier. She recalled the scandal she and Martin had created out of adolescent foolishness. She remembered the awkward year after he arrived back from Europe; the tears shed as she wondered how it would work out. But with amazement she thought back on how they slowly settled into a comfortable rhythm in the hectic but exciting years when their children were young. With gratitude, she remembered the polio scare and the way God used it to lead them to the church that had become so central to her faith and her life.

Anna took a sip of tea and, one more time, glanced back at the page: "But Mary treasured up all these things and pondered them in her heart." The words faded from view as tears welled up in her eyes. She missed Martin. He had loved Christmas and was even more suited than her to the chaos of big family gatherings. But as sad as she was, she also had treasures in her heart. Earlier in the afternoon, she had asked little Ella what her favorite part of Christmas was, and the little one had been to church enough to know the right answer: "Baby Jesus!" Then she added, "And everything else too." Anna chuckled to herself. That's about right. "Baby Jesus . . . and everything else too."

When the last of the tea was consumed, she walked slowly to the kitchen with the empty teacup. Then she violated a rule she'd kept for nearly seventy years. Instead of washing and drying the cup, she turned and walked out of the room, leaving it there for the next morning. She made her way to her bedroom and began to get ready for bed, all the while pondering all these things in her heart.

LET'S TALK

1. When Anna's son Markus contracted polio, a neighbor invited her to a prayer service at her church. Anna and her family weren't regularly attending church at the time. What was it about this new church that felt different to her? What changed in their lives as a result of attending?

2. Despite Anna's sadness at the loss of her husband that year, how do the memories of those years with him bring her comfort? How does the Christmas story and family activities help provide peace despite the loss she's experienced?

CHRISTMAS SLUMP

My recollection of the day is as vivid as a Technicolor movie. It was an impulsive act, one that six-year-old Erik couldn't have fully comprehended at the time, but he turned the Christmas of 1931 into the best we've ever had.

To understand what happened, you need to know a little bit about us. Christmas is a big day in most families, but whatever Christmas represents to your family, multiply it by a factor of ten to understand how we celebrated Christmas. For starters, we're Swedish. Every ethnic group has its cherished traditions, but no one does Christmas better than the Swedes. From Saint Lucia to the smorgasbord, the Swedes have a lock on the best Christmas traditions, food, and sweaters. However, the added extra in our family is that I, Lars Christian Andersson, was born on Christmas Day in 1898. From childhood, Christmas was for me a series of memorable birthday celebrations accompanied by the street decorations the city of Minneapolis thoughtfully put up in honor of my birthday.

When I turned sixteen on Christmas Day 1914, I left the house after lunch with a pair of skates over my shoulder and took a succession of streetcars to Hennepin and Franklin. From there I walked the remaining eight blocks to the Lake of Isles ice rink. While lacing on my skates, I spotted a beautiful blue-eyed blond with an infectious smile. Fate was smiling on me that day, and a cousin introduced me to Ingrid. After a few loops around the frozen surface, I was in love. A tour of duty in France during the Great War as part of the American Expeditionary Forces intervened, but in 1919, Ingrid and I were married in her family's parlor on, you guessed it, Christmas Day. The Christmas theme returned the next year when our first child, Erik's older brother Arvid, was born on Christmas Day 1920. When Inga was born two years later on December 23, it took me weeks to get over the disappointment. Then on June 25, 1925, exactly six months from Christmas, Erik was born.

Times were good when the children arrived. The Great Depression was still a few years away, and blessed with mechanical gifts I'd inherited from my father, I'd done well. At twenty-four, an invention I patented quickly made me rich. When Erik was born, we had a thriving engineering business providing services to food manufacturers like Pillsbury and the Washburn Crosby Company. We bought a large home on Park Avenue, and soon the extended family began to gather with us each Christmas Day. In 1929, life changed for most folks. Our business suffered, but not nearly as much as others did. I'd hired so many relatives that the entire family continued to live well, blessed by the trickle-down benefits that came from the company. In later years, I realized we'd become a pretentious bunch and looked down on those we felt were beneath us. Personally, I began to confuse good fortune with a sense of entitlement.

As it did for all good Swedes, Christmas started for us on the 24th, with a candlelight service at the Lutheran church followed by dinner and then the main act—opening the family Christmas presents. That year I bought Erik an entire set of painted Revolutionary War soldiers, complete with cannons and horses. He was thrilled.

On Christmas morning, Erik woke early to play with the soldiers on the table-sized battlefield I had set up for him in the mansion's library. His mother was already up and at work in the kitchen, beginning preparations for the smorgasbord the entire family would enjoy later in the day. In an hour or so, the aunts, uncles, and cousins would arrive, but for the moment, it was quiet in the house.

"Dad," said Erik, "can I wake up Arvid? I'm bored."

"No," I said. "Let him sleep. He'll be up soon enough." Temporarily thwarted, Erik put on a coat and boots and headed outside to add another wing to the huge snow fort he had built in the corner of the yard near the Park Avenue fence. Something caught his attention at the park across the street, and he walked over to the gate and let himself out. A couple of boys were scavenging for dead branches around the trees. Large homes like ours surrounded the park, but a few blocks away was an area with some desperately poor families. Erik knew a few of the boys from this neighborhood from playing with them in the park the previous summer. I watched as he joined the boys, kicking through a layer of snow, searching for fallen branches that could be used as firewood. Soon his little arms were full of small branches, and he joined them as they left the park and walked in the direction of the boys' home. Ingrid and I shared some anxiety about the influence these boys might have on Erik, but it seemed awkward to intervene, so I let it go. I knew it wouldn't be long before he was back.

Just before he returned, a Model T Ford pulled up in front of the house, and out piled my brother Peter and the rest of his family. Erik arrived back just as my sister Britta and her family, including Erik's cousin Soren, disembarked. Soren is just a year older than Erik, and through the years the two have remained the closest of friends. In a few minutes, the boys were engrossed in a reenactment of the Battle of Bunker Hill with Redcoats falling en masse while just one or two of the Patriots sustained flesh wounds.

Eventually the smells wafting through the house caught their attention, and the boys made their way through the swinging door into the kitchen. There they saw mounds of food piled on every square inch of countertop. There were meatballs, salmon, pickled herring, boiled and fried potatoes, potato pancakes, hard-boiled eggs, a Christmas ham, potatis korv, lingonberries, lutefisk, peas, cabbage, and carrots. And what they couldn't see included the pies, cardamom cake, and cookies laid out on the buffet in the dining room.

Erik asked his mom how they were going to eat all the food. "We can't," she told him. "We won't eat even half of it," she added, turning back to a sizzling pan on the stove.

The boys left the kitchen with a slice of warm bread topped with butter and jam and wandered the house until they came to the entryway. The door opened, and in came Ingrid's sister Christina, her husband, Otto, and their only child, a twelve-year-old girl named Karin. From the adjacent parlor, I could see the door remained open a bit longer than necessary in order for Karin to make a grand and pretentious entrance.

Once Karin shed her coat, she took up her assumed position as the leader of the pack. "We'll play hide-and-seek," she told the seven cousins gathered around her, not giving them a choice in the matter. She listed off the rules, and I heard Erik and Soren complain she took all the fun out of it by making the basement and attic off-limits. At six and seven, Erik and Soren bored of the game before too long and wandered up to the third-floor attic to dig in the storage trunks for buried treasure.

At each end of the attic was a window. The window on the east side looked out over the park. The other looked west toward the neighborhood where Erik's young friends lived. Years later he told me that while Soren rooted through a chest filled with old clothes, he lingered at the window and thought about what he'd seen at the home of the two boys he'd helped to collect firewood. Without a word, he slipped out of the attic and walked quietly down the three flights of stairs to the entryway. Then he opened the closet in the front hallway, took out his coat, slipped it on, stepped into his boots, and walked quickly to the front door. He opened the door, slipped outside, and shut the door quietly behind him.

No one in the house saw him open the front gate and make his way down the block. Soren soon came downstairs to look for Erik but assumed he had rejoined the game of hide-and-seek still in progress.

About twenty minutes later, I happened to glance up in time to see Erik walk up the front walk with his two friends, their parents, a small girl, and an infant in the mother's arms. Christina stood in the entryway, her mouth wide open in shock, as six-year-old Erik marched up the steps with his new friends and opened the front door.

"What is he doing?" she blurted out to no one in particular. The Andersson clan arrived quickly from all four corners of the house about the same time that the last of the guests made their way into the house. No one said a word.

Erik looked up at the grown-ups and said simply, "They're hungry, and we're going to let them eat the leftovers." At first, no one seemed to know quite what to do. Some of the women left the entryway and walked quickly back to the kitchen.

"Erik," Aunt Christina said softly. "Where will they sit?"

"In there," Erik said, pointing to the large dining room table in the room to the left of the entryway.

"But there's not room," she protested.

Sensing we were about to reach an impasse, I stepped forward. "We can put the children in there," I said, pointing to the battlefield table set up in the library.

"Fine," Christina whispered under her breath and walked quickly out of the room.

"Please, folks," I said to the new guests, trying to make an awkward situation a bit more comfortable, "let me hang up your coats." I invited the father, a man named William, to join us in the parlor. Ingrid then invited William's wife, Elizabeth, to join her in the kitchen. Ingrid had Arvid run up to the attic to fetch the old bassinet for the sleeping baby boy. We were still about an hour from dinnertime, but surprisingly, it didn't take the cousins long to incorporate the three older children in their play.

Karin, not particularly known for her flexibility, chose this moment to show a softer side. "Let's go into the music room," she directed. "I think we should put on a Christmas pageant." Access to three more actors gave her the opportunity to cast a full production, including a couple of animals and, most importantly, a live baby for the final production.

Karin's transformation was amazing. When she found out the little girl's name was Mary, she gave her the coveted role and even cast Mary's brother Robert as Joseph. Soon they were deep into the production, with the children learning lines and stage directions. Erik's park friends had only a vague grasp of the story. Robert's brother Jack was proud of his role as a king until he found out he had to bow down to a baby. "What kind of king bows down to anyone?" he said indignantly. "He's supposed to bow down to me!"

In about forty-five minutes, Karin had most of the kinks worked out, and the adults gathered in the music room to see the finished production. The baby, still asleep in the bassinet, was carefully transported to the center of the tableau, and the production began.

"And it came to pass in those days, that there went out a decree from Caesar Augustus that all the world should be taxed," Peter's oldest boy Bjorn recited, doing his best to make his voice as deep as possible. "And all went to be taxed, every one into his own city. And Joseph also went up from Galilee, out of the city of Nazareth, into Judaea, unto the city of David, which is called Bethlehem; (because he was of the house and lineage of David)." Then Joseph and Mary entered from the entryway, Mary seated on Soren, his back draped with a brown piece of fabric designed to make him look something like a donkey.

"He went there," Bjorn continued, "'to be taxed with Mary his espoused wife, being great with child.'" The pageant's Mary dutifully patted the pillow fastened underneath the nearly worn-out nightgown that served as her robe for the production.

The Holy Family made their way across the room to an area near the piano where a stern and serious actor looked down at the couple. "Sir," Robert said, "do you have a place for us to stay in your hotel?"

"Inn," corrected Karin in a low voice. "It's an inn, not a hotel."

"Okay," said Robert. "Is there any place in your inn for us to stay? She's about to have a baby."

"No," said the innkeeper.

Then there was silence. No one said anything until Karin whispered, "The stable."

"Oh yeah," said the innkeeper. "You can stay in the barn out back."

"Stable," corrected Karin.

"Yeah, right," said an annoyed innkeeper. "The stable's round the back."

Mary and Joseph continued their journey, but the delays took a toll on the donkey. When they arrived at the stable, Mary slipped off the donkey's back.

"And so it was, that, while they were there," Bjorn continued, "the days were accomplished that she should be delivered. And she brought forth her firstborn son, and wrapped him in swaddling clothes, and laid him in a manger." Little Mary quickly shed the pillow underneath her nightgown and sat on the small stool Karin had positioned behind the manger.

At that moment, Soren abandoned his posture as donkey and sat down beside the manger. Mary shot him a glare, and Soren, clearly exhausted at how long the journey had taken, said, "Hey, it's not easy being a donkey."

To which Mary shot back, "And you think it's easy being a virgin?"

The men in the room erupted with laughter, followed by the women, who laughed more nervously. The children looked around, puzzled why everyone thought it was so funny.

When the laughter died down, Bjorn began again: "And there were in the same country shepherds abiding in the field, keeping watch over their flock by night." With this, Erik and Soren, this time with white fabric draped over their backs, started to baa and bleat like the sheep they were impersonating. Behind them were two shepherds, one a suddenly transformed former innkeeper. "And, lo, the angel of the Lord came upon them, and the glory of the Lord shone round about them: and they were sore afraid."

Just then, Karin and one of the other girls appeared in white nightgowns with silver ribbons woven in a circle on top of their heads. "Fear not: for, behold, I bring you good tidings of great joy, which shall be to all people," said Karin.

Then the other cousin spoke up: "For unto you is born this day in the city of David a Saviour, which is Christ the Lord."

"And this shall be a sign unto you," Karin continued. "Ye shall find the babe wrapped in swaddling clothes, lying in a manger." Then the two girls joined together, saying, "Glory to God in the highest, and on earth peace, good will toward men."

From the back of the room came the three wise men, crowns on their heads and gifts in their hands. The three, along with Jack, who had had a change of heart, bowed down before the baby and handed Mary and Joseph the gifts.

Karin and most of the audience thought the production was finished, but her Joseph, conflating another biblical story, added something he thought she'd forgotten: "Hey, everybody, shepherds, and kings, go into all the highways and byways and make people come in for the banquet."

"He's right," Ingrid said. "Dinner is served." Everyone applauded and made their way to their respective tables.

At dinner, I had William sit to my right; his wife was at the other end of the table by Ingrid. As it turned out, we were the same age. We'd both served in the Great War. Then he had returned to Minnesota, but the panic of 1920 and 1921 nearly wiped out the family farm near Belle Plaine, so he came to Minneapolis where he secured work in a factory. But with the arrival of the Great Depression, he'd only been able to find temporary work for the last two years. In fact, that morning there was no food in the house. When Erik had arrived at the front door to their apartment, his arms full of the wood they used to heat the home, little Mary had asked him if he had any extra bread to give her.

"I don't think so," he'd said. "We're having company today."

Then before her mother could tell her to be quiet, she'd said, "Do you think there will be any leftovers?" It took an hour or so, but as he looked out the attic window in the direction of his park friends' home, everything came into focus. There was, Erik remembered, more than enough food. So he decided his friends and their family should get a chance to eat the leftovers.

I've thought often about that day and what it meant to our family. In a subtle but profound way, Erik's simple compassionate act changed my life. A few short years of success and I'd grown proud. I thought I deserved all I had. My heart had hardened to the needs of those who suffered in those days. I realized if Jesus could humble Himself to become one of us, then I, too, needed to become humble enough to serve others. I couldn't give my life for the sins of the world, but I could perhaps love others in His name.

The next week I had Erik take me to William and Elizabeth's house. I told William I had a job I needed him to do. Frankly it wasn't quite true, but as it turned out, he was a hard worker, and for the next ten years he was with the company. When William's dad died, he moved back to Belle Plaine to take over the family farm, but our families have stayed in touch through the years.

Earlier that year, a reporter asked Babe Ruth why he had been paid more than Herbert Hoover, the president of the United States. "Well," he said, "I guess I had a better year than he did." When William and I shared a Christmas meal together, we found we shared a love for baseball. What the day showed me is that, like baseball players, every once in a while you go through a slump. In our own ways, both William and I came out of ours on a Christmas Day, thanks to the generosity of a six-year-old boy.

LET'S TALK

1. Erik's father, Lars, is a wealthy man who has come to look down on others who have less than he does. How does Erik's kindness humble him? What does he learn about William and his family that changes his perspective?

2. What does Erik learn from his mother that leads him to invite the family of his friends from the park to Christmas dinner? Do you know of an organization that serves the poor in your city? Perhaps you could make a donation or even help them serve the poor this Christmas season.

SECOND CHANCE CHRISTMAS

This really is a Christmas story, believe me. But to appreciate how remarkable it was that everything turned out as it did, I need to start at the beginning.

In the week before Christmas, Edward P. Slone went to two funerals and a birthday party. It was funerals that got the attention of this tight-fisted, covetous old man, and it was the birthday party and what happened after that changed his life.

The funerals couldn't have been more different. The first was for Jacob Moore, Ed's longtime business partner. They met in their early twenties when both were chasing their first million. Eventually they entered into a partnership that made both men spectacularly wealthy. They shared little in common except a passion for making money, but it was enough to hold them together for decades. A competitor once said of Ed, "He's a lot smarter than people give him credit for, and even meaner than they say he is."

※ ※ ※

Ed entered the smaller of the two chapels in the funeral home. A nearly empty parking lot let him know few even bothered to show up. The funeral director, in a standard-issue navy blue suit, white shirt, and red tie, handed him a program. About twenty people were scattered throughout the chapel. A walnut casket with gold hardware stood conspicuously at the front of the room. A few looked up when Ed entered, and those who knew him personally nodded greetings. He found a seat halfway up the aisle and sat down.

A minister welcomed everyone. It was evident this poor soul had never met Jacob. But he was a professional and said all one should on such an occasion, doing his best to praise Jacob without telling any outright fibs. And, to Ed's relief, he was short and to the point; the service was over in twenty minutes. He then invited the guests to a reception in an adjacent room. A dozen or so filed in where a buffet table held chicken salad on croissants, small bags of potato chips, and chocolate-frosted brownies.

The group sorted themselves out at two tables: one made up of former business associates and the other family. The minister said a short prayer and encouraged them to share stories about Jacob as a way of honoring his memory. His suggestion fell flat because frankly there wasn't much to say. One retired banker Jacob worked with said, "Some people never change. Jerks when they're young; jerks when they're old," and everyone awkwardly laughed. After what Ed hoped was a suitable amount of time, he got up, said his goodbyes, and left.

As he climbed behind the wheel of his black S-Class Mercedes, a sense of sadness gripped him while he drove the half hour to his lakeside estate. Within minutes of his arrival, he was in his home office, grateful for the distraction of a few business issues that had surfaced in the three hours since he'd left home.

Not quite twenty-four hours later he guided his car down a narrow street. The small parking lot at St. Luke's AME Church was full, so he found a place a block and a half away and walked to the building. He tried to slip in the back of the nearly full sanctuary, but an usher approached him and told him the family requested he sit with them. It felt awkward, but he followed the man to a seat in the second row. Several of Bea's children greeted him, and her husband, Carl, thanked him for coming.

Bea Collins started as a receptionist at Green River Industries and quickly made herself useful. After three successive personal assistants had quit on him, he asked her to take the job temporarily. Twenty-nine years later she was still there.

Efficient, reliable, and discreet, she endured his tantrums even though he never apologized. Then one day she announced she'd be retiring at sixty-five. He didn't believe her, but the day after her birthday she handed him a memo with the status of current projects along with a binder with complete instruction on how the job should be done. Then she cleaned out her desk and, at 5:30 p.m., walked out the door. Ed stood there dumbfounded.

The minister, resplendent in a black robe and white stole, ascended to the pulpit. "We have come today not to mourn a death but to celebrate a life," he said to a few scattered "amens." "This is not a day to weep. Oh no, we must not be sad! Today Sister Bea has crossed the River Jordan into the Promised Land. A place where the Lord God Almighty has wiped away every tear and there is no death or sorrow or crying or pain. For He," the minister said, his voice rising, "has made all things new."

"Amens" reverberated throughout the sanctuary. It was clear he was just getting started. "Sister Bea was a woman filled with the Holy Ghost. And now she is in the presence of her Lord and Savior Jesus Christ." Then, knowing Christmas was on everyone's mind, he said, "Where she is today there is no silent night. For the angels in that celestial choir are singing 'Glory, Glory, Hallelujah.'"

When he finished, the choir began to sing, "Soon and very soon, we are goin' to see the King. Hallelujah, hallelujah. We are goin' to see the King. No more cryin' there, we are goin' to see the King."

At the minister's invitation, several came forward to share stories about Bea's kindness and generosity—times she showed up with a meal for a new mom, a check for a light bill, or the offer to take an extra child or two for a few days or even weeks when a family got in a jam. They told how she sat and listened, then gave just the right advice.

Ed was floored. Someone he'd spent so much time with, he barely knew. Yet he remembered all she had done for him, things he now realized he'd never thanked her for. Yet she always did it willingly, graciously, and with kindness.

The choir sang "Amazing Grace": "Yea, when this flesh and heart shall fail, and mortal life shall cease, I shall possess, within the veil, a life of joy and peace." Then they shifted gears, launching into, "Some glad morning when this life is o'er, I'll fly away; to a home on God's celestial shore, I'll fly away. I'll fly away, oh glory, I'll fly away; in the morning when I die, hallelujah, by and by, I'll fly away."

After the minister pronounced the benediction, the entire congregation, as one, relocated to the church basement. And it wasn't chicken salad on croissants for this crowd. There was fried chicken and ribs, with mashed potatoes and gravy and macaroni and cheese. There were greens, okra, black-eyed peas, and cornbread, with peach cobbler for dessert. Ed sat with the family; they insisted. He was at a table with two of Bea's sons. One, he learned, was an attorney with a local firm and the other a manager with a telecommunications company. *How was it,* he thought, *he didn't know any of this?*

❋ ❋ ❋

Walking to his car, he was a jumble of confusing emotions; a mixture of regret mingled with a desire to make amends.

Somewhere in his frontal lobe, he knew he'd experienced something wonderful. But just as quickly, he tried to shut out the thought as he walked the last thirty yards to his car.

❋ ❋ ❋

When he got back to the car, he turned his phone back on and saw a voice mail from his son, Ford. Ed was a largely absent father and divorced Ford's mother during the boy's fourth year of medical school. It was the same year his first grandchild was born, a girl named Sarah. It had been five years before Ed had even met her. She was twenty-one now and in her senior year of college.

The message was an invitation to attend a birthday party for his youngest grandson, Tyler. Ten years younger than nineteen-year-old Brandon, Tyler was turning nine on Christmas Eve and had asked specifically if Grandpa Ed could come. In the message, Ford explained the party started at one, then they planned to have dinner and attend a candlelight Christmas Eve service at their church. His tone of voice suggested he didn't expect his dad to make more than a token appearance.

When Ed finished listening, he thought of Bea's family just a block and a half away; her husband, their five children and spouses, and more than a dozen grandchildren. And in the moment, he made a snap and momentous decision and hit the call back button.

Ford answered on the second ring. "Did you get the message?"

"Yes. And I'll come."

"To the party?" Ford asked, just to clarify.

"No. To the whole thing."

"You mean the party, dinner, and church?"

"Yes," Ed said.

"Okay," said his son, a bit shocked. "Well, I guess we'll see you at one," and they hung up.

Ed had his doubts, but the lingering memory of what he'd experienced created a longing he hadn't felt in a long time. A day later he made another call to his son about what to buy Tyler for his birthday. "An iPad?" he asked.

"No. He already has one."

"What about a flat-screen TV for his bedroom?"

"You're kidding, aren't you?"

They finally settled on a kid-friendly drone, even though Ford knew his wife, Rebecca, might not approve. Ed was shocked he could get one for $100, so he threw in a LEGO Star Wars Episode VIII Heavy Assault Walker building kit for another $175.

❄ ❄ ❄

The night before the party, he had trouble falling asleep. It made him wonder if somehow, in his old age, he was getting soft. Finally, he got up, made himself a snack and flipped channels for an hour. One hundred and fifty-seven channels, he thought, and nothing on. Eventually he felt tired enough to head back to bed. He tossed and turned a bit more before sleeping restlessly until waking a few minutes before his alarm was set to go off.

Ed arrived when preparations for the party were not quite complete. When Tyler's friends gathered, he opened his presents. Half were LEGOs, but Ed was relieved no one else gave him a Star Wars Episode VIII Heavy Assault Walker. And Ford was right; Rebecca wasn't happy about the drone.

The boys ate zucchini brownies, gluten-free chocolate chip cookies, and apple slices. Actually, no one ate the apple slices, and the brownies tasted awful. Ed wondered why Tyler's mother even bothered. What happened to good old birthday cake and ice cream?

Tyler, it turned out, was a fairly typical nine-year-old. His enthusiasm exceeded his judgment, and he said pretty much what was on his mind; there wasn't much in the way of edit. The next couple of hours went fast.

Ed wondered how his son was so normal. He'd been married to the same woman for twenty-five years. His children were reasonably behaved and, from what he could tell, seemed untouched by the maladies many of his peers talked about with their offspring. Here was a house full of well-adjusted human beings, he realized, no thanks to him.

At five, parents arrived to pick up their boys, and as soon as they were all gone, Rebecca rushed Tyler upstairs to get him changed into nicer clothes for the evening. After dinner, Ed offered to drive, so the entire crew piled into black leather-lined Cadillac Escalade as he drove the ten minutes to church.

Other than funerals and an occasional wedding, Ed hadn't been in a church for years. He walked in with Tyler, who seemed to know quite a few people. It suddenly dawned on Ed that this family must attend here regularly, not just on Christmas and Easter.

The church was brightly lit with garland and candles everywhere. The room was nearly full, so they split into two groups with Ed, Tyler, and Ford in one row and Rebecca, Sarah, and Brandon in another.

The choir began with "O Come, All Ye Faithful," then the choir director invited the congregation to stand and sing with them during the second verse. Then they sang "Hark! The Herald Angels Sing" and "What Child Is This?"

When everyone was seated, the minister read the Christmas story while a cast of grade-schoolers acted it out in a series of tableaux. "In those days Caesar Augustus issued a decree," he read, "that a census should be taken of the entire Roman world. . . . So Joseph also went up from the town of Nazareth in Galilee to Judea, to Bethlehem the town of David . . . with Mary, who was pledged to be married to him and was expecting a child.

"While they were there, the time came for the baby to be born, and she gave birth to her firstborn, a son. She wrapped him in cloths and placed him in a manger, because there was no guest room available for them."

He then read about the shepherds, the bright lights, and the angel choir singing, "Glory to God in the highest heaven, and on earth peace to those on whom his favor rests."

When the cast of characters shuffled off the stage, the minister said, "Imagine, if you will, the reaction of the shepherds. When the angel appeared, they were scared to death. So to calm their fears, the angel said, 'Do not be afraid.' And so, in the middle of an ordinary night, an extraordinary God broke into their ordinary lives. Is it not this way with us as well? Doesn't Jesus at times break into our lives when we least expect it?

"This is what the birth of Jesus is all about—God coming down to meet us, not on high holy days, but on the ordinary days, in ordinary places, and only sometimes in extraordinary ways. And when that happens, He says to us what He said to the shepherds: 'Do not be afraid. I bring you good news that will cause great joy for all the people. Today in the town of David a Savior has been born to you; he is the Messiah, the Lord.'"

He paused, looked up, and said, "The good news is God meets us in our pain and loneliness. He meets us in our frustrations and disappointments. He meets us on Mondays and Tuesdays as well as on Sundays. And He offers to be a part of every day of our lives, as ordinary as they might be."

Then he said, "I don't know what you expected when you came here today, but just maybe God is breaking into your life in an unexpected way. It may not be miraculous, but simply the sense there's more to life than what you can see or hear or feel. It's not often an angel choir fills the sky with a music-and-light show. In fact, most of the time it's much more ordinary. But in whatever way He comes, don't push Him aside."

He continued, "At the end the story, it says, 'Mary treasured up all these things and pondered them in her heart.' Perhaps we can follow Mary's example and take time to ponder these things in our hearts. Whatever you do, don't let this moment slip away."

Then everyone joined in singing . . .

Joy to the world, the Lord is come
Let earth receive her King
Let ev'ry heart prepare Him room
And heav'n and nature sing

Tyler stayed awake for most of the service, but toward the end he leaned against his grandfather and fell asleep. At first it felt awkward, but Ed put his arm around the boy and let him nuzzle in. Ford's jaw just about hit the floor.

On the way home, Rebecca asked him if he wanted to join them for Christmas. He was about to give an excuse when he blurted out a yes.

He arrived as instructed at ten o'clock the next morning and was nearly decapitated when Tyler's new drone buzzed by him at neck level. The family gifts were already opened, so Tyler showed his grandfather all his loot.

There was quite a spread at the table: an egg bake, bacon, coffee cake, fruit, and various beverages. The conversation flowed, and even Ed found himself drawn in. Chitchat had never been his thing, but he soon discovered it went a lot better if you asked a few questions.

After everyone had eaten and the dishes were washed and put away, Brandon asked Tyler, in a voice everyone could hear, "Is it time?"

To which Tyler replied, "It's time!" and everyone made their way into the family room. Tyler explained to his grandfather that every Christmas they had to watch the movie *Elf*. When Ed looked puzzled, Tyler said,

"You mean you've never seen *Elf*? Where have you been all these years?" Everyone laughed.

Ed quickly learned that, in this family, watching this zany movie he'd somehow missed in the theaters was quite an experience. All three children had committed whole sections of dialogue to memory. So when Buddy the Elf said, "We elves try to stick to the four main food groups," all three immediately joined Buddy, saying, "Candy, candy canes, candy corn, and syrup." And when Buddy answered the phone in his biological father's office, all three burst out, "Buddy the Elf, what's your favorite color?" And when Buddy asked an angry raccoon, "Does someone need a hug?" all three ran off to find someone in the room to hug. In the end Ed was amazed that something so inane could also be so funny.

After the movie ended, Ed asked Brandon what he was studying in college. "Economics," he answered.

"You don't say," said Ed. "What do you want to do with it?"

"Probably business. Maybe finance."

Shocked he didn't know any of this, Ed said, "We should talk. I might have something for you to do this summer."

Brandon told his grandfather he didn't want anything handed to him, and Ed almost blurted out, "I'd never do that," before he caught himself. "Still," he told Brandon, "why don't you come by the office before you head back to school?" And the two talked dates.

By the end of the afternoon, Ed had also invited Tyler to his estate for a playdate, although he had no idea what he would do with a nine-year-old boy for an entire afternoon. But then, the rest of the family seemed to have no idea what to do with Ed.

"What do you think happened to him?" Rebecca asked Ford when they were alone in the kitchen. "You'd almost think Mr. Grinch met Cindy Lou." They both laughed, but it did seem as if Ed's heart was starting to resemble a normal human heart.

❄ ❄ ❄

The next week Ed and Ford met for lunch. "Dad," Ford said, "this may sound rude, but what's going on? Frankly you've never liked Christmas, and now suddenly you're Clark Griswold."

"Well, I don't know who Clark is," Ed said, "but I had quite a week and decided I need to make some changes. But I'm not quite sure where to start."

Then Ed told his son about the two funerals. And with tears in his eyes—yes, tears, think of it—he told him that Christmas Eve and Christmas Day were the best two days he could remember in a long time. "I left Jacob's funeral with a sense that everything the two of us had done together didn't amount to anything worthwhile. And then, just twenty-four hours later, I hear people praise someone I took for granted. Life's way too short to waste by accumulating more stuff. I may not have much time left, but with the time I've got, I need to do something useful. My life so far has been a series of missed opportunities."

"Good," Ford said, still skeptical. "But you ought to put some thought into this."

"Oh, I have," his dad said. "But I need your help. You're a good man, Ford. A lot better man than I'll ever be. You are kind, forgiving, charitable, and thoroughly decent. And I need to make amends for some of the things I've done and for others I've failed to do. So in the time I have left, I want to be a different man. I just trust I'm not past hope."

Ed said he'd started to make a list of people he wanted to do something for. There was Bea's family—her husband, their children and grandchildren. There was a younger brother, an old college friend, a housekeeper, his accountant, and a neighbor he'd once been close to. He said he also knew he needed to do some good with all his money. Other than make himself comfortable, all he'd ever done was pile it up in bank accounts. It was time, he said, to give some of it away.

"Listen, Dad," Ford said. "I hope you don't take this wrong, because everything you've said so far is great. We should all do what you're doing—no matter how much we have. But I hope you don't think you'll be able to make up for everything in a few weeks. Christmas is a time to think about generosity. So do the good that's in your heart. But I also hope you realize the gift you found this Christmas is that God loves you no matter what's happened in the past."

The two men looked at each other across the table, and Ed realized his son was right. God's grace came to him that Christmas. But still he wanted to get busy. It's all he knew how to do.

LET'S TALK

1. If you've read Charles Dickens's famous story, *A Christmas Carol*, you may see similarities between Ed and Scrooge. Just as Scrooge's dreams get his attention, how do the two very different funerals get Ed's?

2. The pastor said that occasionally God breaks into our lives in unexpected ways. After God gets Ed's attention, Ed tells his son, Ford, about some changes he's going to make in his life. "Good," Ford says. Then he reminds his father there's an even bigger lesson to take away from the Christmas story. What is the lesson? How does it make you feel to know that God loves you no matter what's happened in your past?

THE STORY BEHIND THE STORIES

I've often been asked where I get the inspiration for these stories. The answer is there's no single source. Each fall I begin thinking about the year's story and generally have an idea in hand by Thanksgiving. For many of the stories I can't recall where the idea came from, but there are a few for which I do.

The very first story I wrote, "A Little Christmas Miracle," isn't based on actual events, but does contain one autobiographical anecdote. As a child I was not a fan of Christmas pageants; wearing a bathrobe and a hand towel tied on my head just wasn't cool. So when, as a sixth grader, I was told I had the honor of playing Joseph in that year's pageant, I did as our protagonist did, and secretly tossed both the script and the rehearsal schedule in the trash on my way home from church. The following Saturday morning I was conveniently missing when my mother received a frantic phone call from the director wondering where I was. I don't remember if the result was a demotion to shepherd or wise man, but regardless, I was not disappointed.

Another story, "Ivy's Christmas Visitors," came during a year in which our daughters' school schedules were dramatically different. Aimée, our oldest, was in middle school and had to be out the door at 7:15 am. While Hannah, the youngest and still in grade school, didn't need to catch the bus until 9:00 am. Hannah was an early riser which often left us with an hour or more of time to fill before the bus arrived. One way we used that time was to read together. That year we read several books of fairy tales, which, in turn, inspired my attempt to write a Christmas fairy tale.

"Christmas Slump," a story set in the Great Depression, was inspired by a family visit to the American Swedish Institute in Minneapolis. Housed in the Turnblad Mansion, this museum provides a window into the experience of the early Swedish immigrants to Minnesota. As we toured the mansion I began to imagine a story set in this spectacular home. I don't have an ounce of Swedish blood in me, but there is one month of the year I would love to be Swedish—December. I'm sure it will get me in trouble to say, but, in my opinion, Swedes do Christmas better than anyone else.

"Christmas Refugee" was inspired by an article about young mother who befriended a refugee she met one fall browsing the children's section in a local library. An unlikely friendship blossomed between two women who couldn't have been more different. Changing a few of the details, I imagined how their friendship might have unfolded.

Finally, if it isn't obvious already, "Second Chance Christmas," is a retelling of Charles Dickens' "A Christmas Carol." The year I wrote this story, I reread Dickens' novella and was again moved by the transformation in Scrooge as the story unfolds.

To order additional copies of this book, go to:

johnmsommerville.com